FOUR MONTHS' CAMPING IN THE HIMALAYAS

OUR CAMP BELOW THE SACRED MOUNTAIN OF KAILAS

[Frontispiece.]

FOUR MONTHS' CAMPING
IN THE
HIMALAYAS

W. G. N. VAN DER SLEEN

TRANSLATED
BY
M.W. HOPER

GYAN

Published by

GYAN

Gyan Publishing House
5, Ansari Road
Daryaganj, New Delhi-110002
Phone: 011-47034999, 9811692060
E-mail: books@gyanbooks.com

Distribution Network
gyanbooks.com
India, USA, Canada, UK, Australia, France

ISBN : 978-81-212-3403-0 (PB)
First Published, London, 1929

2nd Impression 2020

Printed at: Gyan Press, Delhi.

FOUR MONTHS' CAMPING IN THE HIMALAYAS

BY

DR. W. G. N. VAN DER SLEEN

TRANSLATED BY

M. W. HOPER

LONDON

PHILIP ALLAN & CO. LTD.

69 GREAT RUSSELL STREET

MDCCCCXXIX

TO HER WHO TAUGHT ME TO TALK
MY MOTHER

FOREWORD

In attempting to set down for my readers some account of our travels, my chief difficulty has been one of selection; for we have visited many countries, and recollections are abundant. But in looking back over a multitude of experiences, our tour in the Himalayas stands out as of supreme importance. So I have given in the following pages a description of our adventures and vicissitudes among these, the highest mountains of the world.

The expedition was undertaken from a general interest in this remarkable region on the confines of Thibet, rather than from a mere love of climbing mountains or of revising maps. In "general interest" I include a desire to become more closely acquainted with the structure of this colossal mountain-system of which, alas, so little is really known that any discoveries made in the course of a short four months' tour are necessarily but a drop in the ocean of knowledge yet to be acquired.

The actual results of our researches into the geological nature of the rocks will have to be worked out in laboratories from the examination of small fragments of laminated strata. The same condition obtains with regard to our explorations in the animal and vegetable world, and more especially those connected with entomology. Nevertheless I have given in this book a few particulars on these subjects which may be acceptable to the general reader. At some future date I hope to have the opportunity of publishing the scientific results of our tour *in extenso.* Meanwhile I venture to hope that the following pages, of capital import to ourselves, may be not without interest to others also.

W. G. N. VAN DER SLEEN.

CONTENTS

PART I

TO THE HIGHEST MOUNTAINS IN THE WORLD

PART II

THE AUTUMN TOUR

ILLUSTRATIONS

PART I

TO THE HIGHEST MOUNTAINS IN THE WORLD

CHAPTER I

SIMLA. PREPARING FOR THE START

SIMLA at last! And now to business. For the next few days we shall be occupied with our preparations for our journey, but with opportunities between whiles of becoming acquainted with the remarkable place in which we find ourselves. Remarkable in every sense. Built on the topmost ridge of a mountain promontory, the European quarter of the town commands a view of incredible beauty. To the south, falling sheer away to the vast and sun-drenched stretches of the plains, veiled after the first clear morning hours in a dusty vaporous haze. Northward, looking through forests of cedar away across the foothills to the great Himalayas, whose lofty glacier-crowned summits are now reflecting the low rays of an afternoon sun, and seem, as day declines, to soar ever higher, ever more sublime, above the gathering evening mists in the valleys at our feet. We shall not easily forget that view from the 'Ridge' nor our walks through the cedar woods after a most gorgeous sunset, while all along the hillside the lights come out clear and sparkling in the mountain air, signs that a twentieth century civilisation has marked this special mountain ridge as her own.

Although Simla lies at the foot of the Himalayas it is none the less 7048 feet above sea level, or three times as high as the Swiss Rigi. A hundred years or so ago it was only an insignificant village of hill-people of the type we shall meet further up country, semi-barbarous and with a modicum of daily needs. But when the British Government handed back most of the surrounding territory to the Native States at the close of the great Gurkha War, it reserved this loveliest of spots for itself and founded a sanitorium here which rapidly became the nucleus of a growing community. In 1864 Simla was chosen as the chief summer residence ot British India, and since then considerations of space alone have limited the increase in population. The precipitous nature of the environs makes it impossible to build except on the plateaux and the outlying mountain spurs, which are almost entirely covered by English country houses, and some even of these appear to have a precarious foothold. The Bazaar, or native quarter, lies clinging on by its eyebrows to the steep face of the rock just below the main street of the European town, so that from the level of the big modern shops and warehouses you can look straight down upon a crowd purely oriental in character. Its swarming masses of humanity comprise every kind of racial type, from the South Indian official to the Thibetan coolie. Oh, that bazaar in Simla! Kipling alone has been able to do it justice and bring home to the unimaginative Western mind in a few vivid sketches the glowing colour of the scene. But it is impossible in Simla to get any insight into the life of the people, the distinction between European and native being too great to allow of any intercourse. For this, one had better go to Bombay or Delhi, or even to Madras, where the educated native is in many respects the social equal of the European.

However, we are in Simla to prepare for our journey,

not to study the habits of the citizens. Our first and chiefest concern is the choice of a servant. We have already felt the need of one even during our hotel life in the larger cities, for servants are *de rigueur* in India. And you don't have to look out for them. They come to you. For instance, every European whose arrival is announced in the Simla papers finds a row of silent figures squatting outside his bedroom door in the morning. They rise and salaam as you appear, and with a murmur of "Salaam Sahib" thrust into your hands a big bundle of letters in which they are described as willing and capable to do anything and everything, and more besides. There is no difficulty in sifting out the first batch, as you instantly dismiss all who are unable to reply in English to an English question. As these generally represent about three-fourths of the applicants one may conclude that education here is not on an exceptionally high level. Then you deal with those that remain, when you discover that a single remark on your part about a dirty shirt or grubby hands is sufficient to relieve you, not only of the case in question, but of several other candidates for your favour as well. The motto: "Know thyself" is evidently as familiar here as with us.

At last only five are left, three of whom have credentials, apparently bought or borrowed, in half a dozen different names. Which brings us to number four. This is a pugnacious-looking Mohammedan with a heavy beard. He looks down demurely, scarce venturing to meet my gaze, but when I dismiss him there is a treacherous glitter in his eyes. I did it to test him. This reduces us to one man. He describes himself as a Christian, speaking timidly and folding his hands in the usual submissive Hindu fashion. But while I am looking at his papers his eyes keep wandering about the room weighing up and measuring every item of our luggage. And when my wife happens to let some money chink in her hand, he gives one quick glance in her direction and drops his eyes again. A humbug with a spurious character! So out with him too!

This makes a clean sweep. But no sooner do we come in from our walk than there is another set of waiting figures. And after lunch yet another, two of whom we order to come back later. And so on at intervals throughout the day. They post themselves outside the door and there they stand, ready with a "Salaam Sahib" whenever you come out.

I may here take occasion to mention that Hindustani as spoken to-day is a peculiar medley made up from the language of the rulers and the lingoes of the ruled. It is the common speech of the country from Calcutta to Karachi, from Simla to Bombay. The older languages, however, notably Tamil and Telegu, still prevail in the South, while a large proportion of the Hindustani-speaking natives all over India continue to make regular use of their own vernacular among themselves. This is presumably the reason why the values on the banknotes are given in no less than nine different languages—though I am bound to add that throughout my journey I never met a soul who could tell me so much as the name of any one of them.

We are busily occupied packing our trunks when there comes a knock at the door. I look up. Surely not a native? He wouldn't dare. Another knock. This is really the limit! "Well!" I cry, "come in! What's the matter?" Enter a smart fellow. Slim build. White turban. European coatee, and shirt worn inside the trousers—the true Hindu wears his outside—but the trousers themselves are of the Hindu type, long and fitting closely to the leg from the knee. He has left his low shoes outside and stands at attention, a row of military ribands on his breast. He thinks perhaps the Sahib may be wanting a servant? Someone who is accustomed to camping in the hills? The young monkey had taken in our tents at a glance, as he told us later on. A few enquiries elicit the fact that he has some knowledge of the district, though he at once admits that he has not travelled in certain parts. He seems open and straightforward, and can look you in the face anyway. Heels together. Hands to side. I have never been keen on soldiers, but they certainly know how to hold themselves. "Have you got your credentials?" "Yes, sir." "Borrowed any from your comrades?" At this the rogue actually laughs. Laughs if you please full in the face of his future lord and master. And then he glances at my wife. He has a magnificent set of teeth. . . .

The letters are short and to the point, so it ends by our engaging him for three days on trial. If he proves satisfactory he is to go with us to the hills. He asks a modest wage, in our opinion anyway, and instantly displays a wonderful set of accomplishments. With a vigorous rousting in three languages, he drives all the other competitors out of the compound; takes the brush out of my wife's hand and tidies up our clothes, which he folds and carefully puts away; moves one of the boxes for my wife, and while doing so noses round for the boot-brush; hangs the blankets up to air and, in short, makes himself thoroughly at home. When the luncheon bell rings he offers to mend our stockings if my wife has any wool. His own needle he has brought with him stuck into his turban.

After lunch we send him on errands and he brings back his accounts made out in Urdu, dictating the bill to my wife, as he writes English with difficulty. Will the Mem-Sahib add it up for him? And so he went on during the whole tour. He would jot down his expenses in a kind of cuneiform script and then dictate rows, yards long, of items at a penny and a halfpenny, always leaving the addition and payment to us with the utmost confidence. After the first day Santoo, as he called himself, had so won our hearts that we trusted him to engage the rest of our staff for the journey. Oh dear yes, he'd thought of all that! We should need a cook, and a second servant to assist himself and the cook. We must also have a coolie to carry round the bottles at meals on the march, to fetch wood and draw water, etc. By the next day all the said gentlemen were introduced to us. The second servant, who later on turned out to be his brother-in-law, was a great lusty young fellow with a friendly smile, who seemed pleased with everything and afterwards proved to be a regular Jack-of-all-trades. Then there was Tara the cook, in a violet waistcoat and white trousers, carrying an ebony walking-stick with a silver knob and beaming all over with such a sense of conscious worth as was enough to make us engage him three times over. Later on it transpired that Tara had never cooked a meal in his life and had only been brought along because he was such good company. However, we were none the worse for it. It all made for an excellent spirit among the servants, and

SIMLA
An Outpost of Civilisation

OUR TENT
Santoo Has Just Laid the Breakfast

(Face p. 8.)

THE KITCHEN FIRE
MULE DRIVER SMOKING THE HUBBLE-BUBBLE

SEDUM ON THE ROCKS

Jittoo, the second servant, himself was a cook who could even give my wife points, while later it turned out that Santoo also had a cookery book of his own.

Our staff was now complete down to the coolie whom we engaged at the last moment. Meanwhile I had spent several hours in the office of the Deputy-Commissioner-Superintendent-of-the-Hill-States, the highest official personage in the place, who knew the parts we intended to visit pretty well, and so was able to give us much useful advice. He also suited the action to the word by furnishing us with introductions to various native rulers and rajahs and to other English officials who were most courteous in providing us with the newest maps and with permits to put up at the various dâk-bungalows and rest-houses provided for Government officials. The permission of the Deputy-Commissioner was also necessary before we could hire the four mules and two drivers we required from the Government supplies. I really cannot speak too highly of the kind help I received from all officials on merely presenting my card. All this, added to our own and our servants' experience in travelling, and last but not least to the assistance of our friend Mr. J——, the ornithologist, enabled us within the space of a week to have the whole caravan ready to start, and it was gratifying to find at the end of the first day's march, which we purposely made a short one, that nothing seemed to have been forgotten. Our outfit was equal to all emergencies, thanks in great measure to the Dutch "Tourists' Camping Club," whose efficiency has not hitherto been sufficiently appreciated. They had supplied our tents with a sewn-in ground sheet and mosquito-net doors, rendering them better adapted for a sojourn in the tropics. We were also very much pleased with the light weight of our kit, though of course in choosing a camping-ground one had always to bear in mind that it was not proof against storms of the first magnitude on the high mountain ridges. But then an experienced traveller does not generally pitch his tents in such places. It is not worth scaling lofty mountains to seek experiences, however pleasant, at the risk of spending weeks on end in a world of snow, stones and ice.

The chief object of our tour was to study the geological formation of the Sutlej Valley, to collect the interesting minerals that one might expect to find there, and to make a general survey and record of any facts worth noting about this little-known district. For this Valley of the Sutlej, through which, mark you, runs the main road from Hindustan to Thibet, is still comparatively unexplored. The geological atlases merely show it as a blank, or at any rate did so show it, for some few alterations have been made on more recent maps. In scientific literature this tract of country has been treated with scant courtesy, the main reason probably being that its formation is monotonous, yielding nothing of geological interest. The flora of the district immediately around Simla is fairly well known, but as regards the fauna all that has appeared is one list of birds. To which, by the way, we were able to add about a dozen new species. So, all things considered, there seemed to be sufficient reasons for traversing just this special bit of territory, so close to civilisation and yet so unfamiliar to the outside world. There is, besides, much to see and enjoy in long journeys through this region.

SIMLA. PREPARING FOR THE START

As everyone knows, the Himalayas are the highest mountains in the world. But one peculiarity which seems to have escaped general attention is that the great rivers of India, the Indus, the Sutlej and the Bramapootra, rise behind the main Himalayan chain and break their way through these mountains to the great plains and the sea in ravines of indescribable depth. Scientists are pretty well agreed that this can only be explained in one way, namely, by assuming the rivers to be older than the mountains, so that when the latter were formed the sources of the rivers were also raised. This caused an increase of speed in the current, consequently the scooping-out of the river bed took place more rapidly than the corresponding rise in the river bottom. Only by cutting a deeper and deeper channel for themselves in the steadily upheaving mountains could the Sutlej and the Indus have created the enormous ravines through which they now rush down the southern slopes.

This leads me to say a few words on the genesis and development of this mighty chain of mountains. The Himalayas are more or less co-eval with the Alps, the Atlas Mountains, and the Caucasus. In other words they are still young, geologically speaking, being formations of the Tertiary Period. The first distinct theory of the actual origin and growth of mountains was supplied somewhere about 1910 by Wegener. He came to the conclusion that our continents probably had much the same form throughout the geological periods, but that their position on the earth's surface was liable to displacement. The south-easterly drift of the Euro-Asiatic blocks, meeting with immense opposition at certain points, caused a powerful upthrust of the moving mass, thus producing folds in portions of the earth's crust. In this way the Pyrenees, Atlas Mountains, Alps, and Caucasus arose from the impact of Europe with Africa. Similarly, when Hindustan came into contact with some obstacle unknown at the bottom of the ocean, the hitherto low-lying northern portion of the peninsula was thrust together into innumerable folds resulting in the greatest and loftiest mountain system in the world. A great pressure is still going on from the north, of which the numerous earthquakes in the region of the Himalayas are a sign. The intensity of the pressure is evidenced by the tremendous deformation of the rocks exposed to it, instances of which may be seen on every hand in the nullahs and ravines, where great bare walls of rocks are exposed, devoid of all vestige of vegetation.

Previous to the rise of the Himalayas, a shallow sea existed between the old granitic-basalt plateaux of Hindustan and the great Thibeto-Mongolian plain, being part of the Tethys, the primeval Middle Sea which stretched from Mexico to the Pacific Ocean. This flat and relatively thin portion of the earth's crust was peculiarly liable to fold when subjected to horizontal thrusting. Consequently, in the northern and southern foothills of the Himalayas we find everywhere the lime and sandstone strata which were formed some millions of years ago on the bottom of the sea. The best place to study these deposits is the famous Spiti Valley close to the Thibetan frontier, but you meet with them also on the south side of the range. In the upheaval of the Himalayan chain, the rock deposits were subjected, first to an upthrust and then to a rifting process which threw them to either side of the main chain where we find them to-day, mostly at a sharp gradient.

Simla stands on a layer of shale, most of which was probably formed in the carboniferous period at the bottom of the sea, though next to no recognised remains of marine life are ever found here. This shale formation is very monotonous, and extends along the mountains in a band several miles broad. Above it, or rather lying obliquely against it, is a wide belt of limestone which in its turn is covered by tertiary and quaternary strata of sand, clay and gravel. Below the Simla shale—that is, further into the great mountain chain—comes the gneiss-granite of which the centre of the range is composed, except in those places where it joins the strata of primeval rocks. These latter are considered by many to represent the once fluid earth in its first stage of coagulation. In other words, the central granite is relatively recent, having been thrown up in the Tertiary Period from a great depth in a liquid state, when by heat and pressure it considerably transformed the older rocks with which it came into contact. In the contactual zones you will find so-called 'contact' minerals produced by chemical action, among them garnets and tourmalins. The lovely crystals of these interesting minerals are a welcome change to the eye after travelling for days through masses of grey granite. One of these tourmalins by the way, about four inches long, very nearly cost me my life. But of this anon.

Now just a word or two about the map of our route. Thanks to the work of Sven Hedin and other explorers, the whole of Asia, as most people are aware, has now been carefully mapped, though not perhaps with the precision we are accustomed to in our own ordnance maps. With regard to the British portion of the Himalayas, the military maps and those of the Forest Service are very fairly reliable. At any rate they give the positions of the chief peaks, glaciers and rivers pretty accurately, though sometimes a path that has had to change its course owing to one of the frequent earthquakes will be still marked on the wrong side of the stream.

The road from Simla to the Shipki Pass runs at first for a considerable distance across a high mountain ridge, thence descending to the valley ar ' taking you a few days' march along the river. Then uphill and down again to cross the stream with a rise on the other side of over 11,000 feet. Only a small portion of the road lies in the valley itself, fortunately for us; for the temperature there is unpleasantly high. At Chini, the point where the Sutlej cuts its way through the heart of the great Himalayan chain, we climbed on either side of the river to a height of nearly 19,000 feet.

Of these our mountain journeys, and our adventures on and off the beaten track, let the following pages tell.

CHAPTER II

ALONG THE HINDUSTAN-THIBET ROAD

June 4. 6 *a.m.* We find on emerging from our bathrooms that the boys have already brought out the luggage, and the four mules stand ready swishing their tails. The drivers, who are quietly sitting on their heels smoking their hookahs, spring up as we come out. We order the baggage to be corded up in carrying mats and loaded on to the animals, meanwhile seizing the opportunity to take a hurried breakfast, and at 7 o'clock the whole caravan is under way. We start off up the ridge at a slow mountaineering step, altering our pace presently on finding that the first miles of our road are comparatively easy. This is actually the case for the first 50 miles on a march of some days; for the gradients are inconsiderable until after you have passed Narkanda.

It is a glorious summer morning. But we have not gone many steps before we have to reverse our first hasty impressions of Simla and its surroundings. We had come up from the big cities Agra and Delhi, from an atmosphere heavy with heat and thick with human traffic, and had rushed by train through the arid stretches of the plains where the dust of past months swirled in the wind to settle low again in the turbid air. So that on reaching Simla we had breathed again. But once beyond the pine-woods on these barren southern slopes our thermometer is up again at 107° F. in the shade, *i.e.* more than blood heat. Fortunately we are prepared for this, having reduced our clothing to the barest minimum of one indispensable undergarment, a sports shirt or blouse, and a pair of khaki knickers, leaving the knees free. In addition, for the first few days we wore stockings for the sake of appearance, but later on we only had socks in our shoes. The great advantage of this light attire was that it gave scope to the free action, and I may add development, of the muscles of the legs and respiratory organs.

The weather that first morning was really heavenly. Our road ran along a western slope through dense woods of cedar and pine, where the coolness of the mountain night still lingered. In the more open places the cedars gave way to holm-oaks and rhododendrons, the latter growing, not as with us in bushes, but in the form of trees of a size not inferior to the oaks. Though the height of the flowering season was over many of these were still in full bloom, flushing the hillside with colour, and among the great red blossoms hung myriads of bees and bumble-dores busy at their work of pollination.

It was like springtime all along that shady slope. The grass was carpeted with flowers. There were sedums in the crannies of thc rocks, butterflies on the hillside, and birds in the woods; tits and woodpeckers and long-tailed pies as well as paroquets. At every moment there was some new and lovely thing to look at. At every turn the cye was attracted by views deep down into the valleys or away over a succession of mountain ridges to the lofty snow peaks in the distance. The people too were new to us. They cxhibit a type markedly distinct from that of the town-dwellers in the plains, and before long we came

ALONG THE HINDUSTAN-THIBET ROAD

(Face p. 16.)

QUARTZITE ROCKS WITH DWELLING AND NOMAD TENTS

to the actual hill-people in their garments of coarse homespun, the women adorned with a wealth of silver ornaments representing the entire riches of the family. For safes and strong boxes are as unknown here as banking accounts and cashiers! After a while the road makes a bend around the watershed and crosses to the south-east side of the hill. Here there are no longer any cedars or oaks, no rhododendrons nor even any greensward. The hillside indeed looks quite bare from a distance, but at closer quarters one finds there is some scant vegetation, half parched by months of relentless sunshine. It is beginning to get very warm, though warm is a mild term for it. It is more like entering an oven with the heat striking you full in the face. But it is not the miserably enervating heat of the plains, where your pores are choked with dust, the air is saturated with the exhalations of the soil and the odours of man and beast, and where the sweat streams from your face and body even when you lie stretched out in your lounge chair. Up here the air is at any rate free from dust, and there is a certain freshness about it while you are in motion. And after all " a pleasant thing it is for the eyes to behold the sun ! "

The first day's march is a short one of eight miles only, which nevertheless it takes us nearly five hours to do, so constantly are we attracted by some new and unfamiliar sight. Sometimes it will be the caverns in a rock betokening an origin in the depths of primeval seas; or it may be one of the many hundreds of lizards that abound everywhere; or again, a flock of merry tits, white and yellow cole-tits among them, both with the familiar little black choker and a large crest on the head. We camp on a hilltop by a pond in the pine-woods and I make the servants sit down in a semi-circle on the stones, while my wife and I put up the tents just to show them how it is done. It is a treat to see their looks of astonishment as our mansion rises from the ground in a quarter of an hour. But we very soon discovered that they had so little knack of the thing that we continued generally to pitch our tent for ourselves. On one occasion I remember we had gone off to reconnoitre immediately after arrival at a camping ground; on our return we found that the servants had actually contrived to do the job in one hour and a half! They are excellent fellows and as willing as can be. But you can hardly ever teach a Hindu anything. Nor many of our own countrymen for that matter! Otherwise, everything seemed in order. Nothing had been forgotten, and seldom have I experienced such a sense of opulent contentment as I did that day in the mansion which was to be our shelter during months of wandering.

Our home is an ordinary hut-tent of about six and a half feet square, but with the addition of a flannel ground-sheet which is covered by a Kashmiri rug of white goat's hair wool embroidered with a branched pattern of red flowers and green leaves. The canvas trunks with our clothing stand on either side and our knapsacks lie at the entrance. Round the corner, close to the sloping roof, are barrels containing maps, writing materials, etc. Our children's photographs are on the wall, and overhead is the Dutch flag, an emblem totally unknown here. Few natives seem to realise that Holland is anywhere near England. At the back, carefully rolled up, are our sheets and eider-downs, a bundle of underclothes serving temporarily for pillows, while behind the tent, under the pent-house formed where the storm-flap meets the ground, is our so-called 'box-room,' providing us with ample accommodation for the morning bath.

Here I may add a few more particulars about our outfit. Of course we carry with us as few clothes as possible: just a hill-climbing rig-out and not much in the way of underlinen, for we can get that washed by the servants every day and it dries quickly enough in the sun. A topee is always necessary, except in the dense forests, and even there it behoves one to be careful. Smoked spectacles are particularly indispensable. On the occasions when we, my wife especially, suffered from a touch of sunstroke, it was nearly always owing to the glare of intense light on the eyes. Two other items we were of course never without: our field-glasses and our cameras. We were each armed with a pair of Trieder binoculars and a Brandsma reflex camera of 9 × 2 cm., specially adapted for tropical work, an Erneman folding camera 6½ × 9, and a pocket camera 4½ × 6. We also had a compass, but I am one of those happy mortals who has about as much use for such an article as a carrier pigeon or a bird of passage. My watch, or chronometer, seldom differed more than two hours from the actual solar time, which we ascertained at intervals by observing the shortest shadow of one of our tent-poles. Beyond our tent was that of our assistant, Mr. G. Traanberg, a hut-tent similar to ours but smaller, being only 6 ft. × 4 ft. and having no extra ground-sheet or weather-flap. Its occupant, however, found it a thoroughly satisfactory shelter throughout the tour.

We three composed the European contingent of the party. The servants' tent was always pitched some couple of dozen yards away and carefully to leeward. Here the mules were picketed, each animal having one of its hind-legs tethered to a stake with a heap of grass or straw round it. The mule-drivers slept close alongside, rolled up in their blankets. When we got further up into the hills these two rascals always lit a huge fire in the evening, round which they would sit talking till it was out, when they rolled themselves up in their blankets and lay right down on the hot ashes. They also had a clever dodge of heating the side of a rock, against which they would snuggle down and go to sleep. The servants' tent was of the 'A' or wedge type, without a front or back flap, measuring about 8¼ ft. × 3½ ft. and 3½ ft. high. The cooking-stove was always kept here, and Santoo and Jittoo and the cook and the coolie all slept on the top of it, the two mule-drivers also joining the party later on when there were signs of rain.

One more official personage was added to our camp when we got higher up into the mountains, in the shape of a Chuprasi, a kind of general factotum, lent us by the Rajah of Bashahr. So altogether we were a large party and all excellent friends.

The cook had his kitchen next the servants' tent. It consisted of two or three wood fires between big stones on which he set his saucepans, another fire for the meals of the three servants, a separate one for the coolie, and another for the mule-drivers. So we got plenty of fumes

But our real reason for always trying to keep to windward of the servants' quarters was not only the hotchpotch of smells arising from the mules and the fires, from the kitchen and the latrines: it was the hubble-bubble. This is an instrument of torture if you like! I may say here that I bear an inherent grudge against Columbus for having discovered the country whence comes the fragrant weed; but the smell of this water tobacco-pipe far exceeds that of the very worst English cigarette. This is probably because the damp tobacco which is put in the upper part of the pipe is often kept smouldering by lumps of cow-manure, the only available fuel in many parts of the country. In the hills, however, they always used embers from our fire. The mingled fumes are sucked down under the water into a receiver, producing the bubbling sound from which the instrument takes its familiar name. The big Turkish pipes, monsters a yard high and often made of silver cunningly wrought, are seldom met with in the hills. Many mule-drivers, however, have pipes with lovely copper containers, with two stems attached to them of bamboo or cane. To one of these is fixed a stone pipe-bowl as big as a tea-cup, while the smoke is drawn through the other. Travellers on foot generally use a small cocoanut instead of the heavy copper pot. It answers the purpose equally well and is more handy to take up at any odd moment. The pipe is always passed round at the camp fire, but only the owner thereof may put his lips to the mouthpiece. Everyone else must draw through the hollow of the hand.

We three Europeans generally took our meals in front of, or just inside, the big tent, and if the evenings were cold we would often sit for half an hour with the servants over the fire, on which occasions the best rugs would be spread in our honour. 'Baby Sahib,' as they called Traanberg to distinguish him from 'Bara Sahib' or 'great lord,' my own proud self, ventured several times to take a pull at the pipe of peace. My wife and I generally kept well to windward of it.

Our first days speed pleasantly. Our plan is to start in the morning and walk a good distance from 6 to 11. Then the tents are pitched and our things arranged, and we have luncheon. We rest till between 1 and 3, and as the sun declines take another good tramp up or down hill to collect geological and other specimens, and to take a general look round and enjoy ourselves. Now and then we take a day off, at least the mules do. We ourselves seize the opportunity of making a longer excursion than usual to some distant point of interest. We thus spent five days in doing the forty miles which on our return journey in mist and rain we traversed in two. Forty miles, ninety kilometres, five days. This was ample time for us to become at home in our new surroundings. Meanwhile we determined to take everything as it came, to be quietly observant, and to record by pencil or camera any unusual incident that came our way. All the same, by the time we got to Narkanda after again crossing the watershed, and the great cedar forest had engulfed us, we had some moments of secret qualms. Fortunately we had one another to confide in.

In Narkanda our camp was delightfully ensconced among the great cedars on a little terrace about three hundred feet below the level of the road. We had just finished pitching the tents, always a great business, and the baggage being now finally arranged and the fire burning under the kettle, peace once more prevailed in the forest and we gradually yielded ourselves to the heat and stillness of the summer day. But not for long, however. While waiting for tea we had taken out a bunch of bananas to moisten our thirsty throats a little. Whether caused by the sight of these delicacies or the discomfort of the wood smoke I know not, but at that moment a remarkable performance took place in the trees overhead. There was a yelping, screaming and chattering, a darting of grey shadows to and fro, a plunging of heavy bodies from branch to branch, and a rain of twigs, fir-cones, and pine needles upon the tautly drawn tent-roof. And behold, if you please, a troop of some thirty large langurs, grey apes with long tails, spruce black noses and white frilly whiskers, watching what is taking place in their woods. We had not noticed them before, so absolutely still had they been sitting. But now I suppose the sight of the bananas had caused them to lose all self-control, and they were in such a state of excitement that we had to drive them off with a charge of small shot. After a while I slipped after them along the steep hillside and amused myself watching them as they gambolled and romped together, and engaged them in a few games of hide and seek which they seemed thoroughly to understand.

We often came across apes in the Himalayas. These langurs are mostly found in the larger trees, the smaller baboons in the more cultivated parts or where the arable and forest lands meet. Both species are distinguished by the incredible brutality they exhibit towards men and dogs. Occasionally they will show some respect for anyone carrying a gun, but as a rule they don't care a rap for anybody, being sacred creatures. No Hindu will injure an ape if he can help it, and anyone who wishes to remain on good terms with his servants will shoot wide of the mark.

The origin of the sacredness of the ape is a remarkable story, and as it gives a somewhat different view of the religion of the Hindus and their sacred books from that prevailing with us, I will give it in detail.

The Hindu religion has had many prophets. At divers times in history, a son of the Supreme Being has appeared on earth as a man among men, possessing a variety of divine attributes, such as exceptional strength and beauty, which attributes can be increased or discarded at will. One of the most famous of these prophets was Rama, whose life is recorded in the *Ramayana*, or new testament, so to speak, of the Hindus, and who is supposed, according to the latest results of historical research, to have lived in South India six or seven hundred years before the Christian Era. Now it came to pass that Sita the wife of Rama was abducted by the King of Ceylon, who carried her off in a fiery chariot drawn by vultures, having previously, by a ruse, enticed away Rama and his brother.

On discovering that his wife had disappeared Rama called in the assistance of Hunuman, the King of the Apes, to whom he had previously done some service, to help him find her. Hunuman sent out all his subjects, at first in vain. Then he decided on a bold move. With one daring leap he crossed the narrow straits between India and Ceylon and found the long-lost Sita in the garden of the king, who is described as a kind of demon with thirty-two heads, etc. Hunuman sets the town in flames and returns to bring Rama tidings that Sita is waiting for him. Rama immediately starts for Ceylon, accompanied by the apes carrying stones. With these they build a bridge over which his army passes. In pictures of the incident in South India the army of the apes, attired in smart red bathing-drawers, are represented helping him to retrieve

HUNUMAN, KING OF THE APES

Sita. Hunuman in reward for his services is promoted to the number of the gods, and under the title of 'god of faithful servants' has a place of honour in every temple. Historians have identified this memorable campaign with the conquest of Ceylon by the Brahmins. Anyway, all apes have been held sacred ever since.

Returning to camp I find awaiting me the Postmaster-Postman-Headschoolmaster-Undermaster-Mayor-Magistrate and Municipal - Provincial - and - Government - Tax - collector, all rolled into one in the person of the only English-speaking villager. He has ordered an armchair to be brought from the post-office for the Mem-Sahib, one of the three specimens of such official furniture extant between Simla and the Thibetan Frontier. For all ordinary purposes these natives spend their life on the ground, as do very many even of the more enlightened Hindus in the towns. Our visitor is followed by a servant with a basket of cocoanuts. And now came a whole string of requests, the first of which tickled our fancy not a little. It seemed that a few days ago a black bear had come down at early dawn and had picked the apricots in the garden just below his house. Would the Sahib kindly shoot him ? I was only too delighted, of course. So in the evening we got the rifle ready for action and waited for the bear. No tidings of his approach, however, came either that night or the next, so we decided to visit the robber in his own domain. But before doing so there were other questions to be answered. Some of the school-children needed attention, which meant doses of cascara for the most part, and one of them had a horribly festered foot which I treated with a strong application of Peruvian Balsam. These, by the way, were only the first of our patients, for after that throughout our tour scarcely a day passed without our having some sick, infirm, or maimed creature coming to us for help. Fortunately we had reckoned upon this contingency, and thanks to my having filled our medicine chest on the way from stores provided by the Rajah, and some we managed to get sent up from Simla, we were able to help in many cases, and in some instances of blood-poisoning to avert certain death. This is perhaps one of the reasons why we were always so well received by the natives even in those places where the respect due to Englishmen is utterly unknown, from the simple fact that no Englishman ever goes there. Our Santoo, who once for a short time had been a hospital orderly, was, I think, guilty now and then of exaggeration with regard to my skill. We nearly died of laughing at the amount of palaver and gesticulation that he employed when giving out my simple prescriptions to the patients. And important news spreads very rapidly from mouth to mouth in these regions.

To return to the 'postman'—as our letter-carrier, we prefer this one of his many titles. He had still one more request to make. Would we photograph his wife? And on our agreeing he showed himself most solicitous that her wrist-watch should come out properly in the photo, as he said it was the only wrist-watch in the state!

A day or two later we started off to the great haunt of bears, a large ravine formed by one of the tributaries of the Sutlej, the Rajah of Kunmarsain, himself a sufferer from the depredations of the above-mentioned black bear, sending with us his head huntsman and a tracker.

It was a pretty stiff climb. First we followed the tracks of a deer up the side of a hill. Then on and up till we were far above the level of the footpath. Once our guide hurled a stone down into the gully to find out if deer were lurking there, and we saw a yellow shadow swish down through the bushes. Our scrutiny of the ground revealed the spoor of a good-sized panther. The spot where he had lain and scratched himself was covered with the usual black, yellow and white hairs. Presently we descended towards a piece of arable land. There was a big wild figtree standing on the edge of this ground only a few hundred feet away, and my attention was suddenly attracted to a dark object among the branches. Just as I was stepping aside to get a better view of it, a huge black bear dropped plump down out of the tree, bringing after him an avalanche of twigs and pebbles, and scuttled off up the hillside before I had even time to raise my rifle. Pursuit was of course out of the question. When once these animals are disturbed they are so tremendously on their guard that Old Shatterhand of Winnetou alone would be a match for them. I may here mention that this is practically all I saw of the larger beasts of prey during our entire trip, though we often found traces of where they had prowled round our camp during the night, and sheep and goats were killed on several occasions quite close to us by leopards during the daytime.

But quite apart from questions of game that expedition was glorious. Now scrambling, now sliding, we cut obliquely along the side of the hill, where open grassy spaces alternated with cedar woods, a low undergrowth of bamboo forming in places an impenetrable jungle. We sighted another couple of deer, and down by the brook a few antelopes. But the only spoils of the chase was a magnificent snake-eating eagle. I forgot to mention that by another courtesy of the British Government we were supplied with a complete set of shooting licences, which of course we used only for the purpose of securing specimens or for providing ourselves with means of subsistence.

During this hunting excursion we came across some exceptionally interesting rock formations. Down in the bed of the stream, and just below our camp, there is a layer of shale, which hereabouts is full of glittering garnets, an indication that we are nearing the heart of the Himalayas. And when we climbed from Narkanda camp to the summit of Mount Hattu, one of the highest peaks of the mountain spur, we found for the first time, at 10,500 feet, genuine examples of crystalline rocks as well as some ocellate gneiss similar to that found in the Alps. This is a kind of gneiss rock whose stratification exhibits dark micaceous folia with occasional examples of felspar crystals both angular and rounded in shape, and often several inches long. In English these rocks are generally termed gneissose granite. They form the principal component of the part of the Himalayas which we visited, and extend from Narkanda to the Shipki Pass, only interrupted here and there by a few blocks of the older slate deposits, such as quartzite and phyllite.

I have said that Mount Hattu has an elevation of 10,500 feet. So, as our camp was 8700 feet, it was a comparatively short walk to the summit. I have once been at an equally high altitude in the Alps after a terribly exhausting tramp of seven hours through snow and ice. And on one other occasion in Holland. . . . But that time it was in an aeroplane; not a bad idea, by the way, if you want to see half the country in a twinkling.

The way to Mount Hattu rises at first by imperceptible degrees through cedar woods and then at a steeper gradient through groves of ilex. The last few hundred feet are very steep indeed and by a path scarce worthy the name. But it is nice and flat when once you get to the top. And there is a profusion of flowers, especially ranunculuses and thyme, interspersed with dodder weed, the latter proving quite as attractive as the actual flowers to a host of lovely butterflies. We noticed among them the swallow-tail, the clouded yellow, the blue argus and cabbage white. They were of course of a different variety from ours, but with such a distinct family resemblance that the familiar names at once rose to our lips. We were very much struck by this during our tour here in the hills. During our previous wanderings, in the sun-stricken African deserts, the well-nigh barren coral islands of the Red Sea, and the great plains of tropical India, all the animals and plants were quite unknown to us, not only in species, but as representing whole natural orders which have no European equivalents. But here in the Himalayas we felt more or less at home directly. Here there are cedars and other conifers, ranunculuses and buttercups, these mostly of a white variety, columbines, the little wild orchis (Ophrys), sedums, primulas, wild cherries and pears. And it is the same with the birds, beetles and butterflies, and everything that creeps or flies along the sunny hillsides. A good idea of this 'palæarctic' flora and fauna may be gained by remarking how all forms of life throughout the vast expanses of Europe and Asia are, except in the tropical and subtropical areas, much the same in the main. That is to say they are all members of the same natural orders with a similarity of form plainly suggestive of a common ancestry. And just as the Hindus can boast an Indo-

European or Aryan origin, so it is with the animal and vegetable life of the Himalayas.

I am afraid 'the schoolmaster is abroad' in the foregoing remarks. The fact is I have so much to tell from the immense amount of information gathered on our tour that I sometimes almost forget to mention the beauties of the scenery.

I have always had a love of mountain tops. The longer time I can spend in these high places of the earth, and the more untrammelled the view, the better pleased I am. Up here on Mount Hattu one has indeed the feeling of space to turn round in. To the south lie the foothills, a succession of ridges separated by deep chasms, gradually descending ridge by ridge to the level of Simla, an altitude of about 7048 feet, and then making a sudden drop to the plain where lakes and rivers gleam silver in the sunshine. East and west, right and left, are deep ravines with intervening mountain steeps, the northern and western declivities clothed with dense cedar forests, the southern and eastern barren, save for a sparse covering of herbage scorched by exposure to the devastating rays of a subtropical sun. A chequered foreground of dark greens and tawny yellows, sharply defined like the squares on a draughtboard, stretches forth and fades mistily away into that translucent violet-blue that speaks of distance, gradually melting at last on the southern horizon into the azure of the sky. Away to the north, the eye detects a sharp white line as of demarcation, a line growing ever broader and more distinct as it approaches the northern point of the compass from east and west, and slowly resolving itself into the forms of a long series of snow mountains, till it suddenly mcrges into a group of glaciers quite closc at hand, the Shrikan Dhar, only fifty miles away. So mighty are thesc giant heights, so vast their glaciers and so clcar is the atmosphere, that the fissures and clefts, the precipices and ice hummoeks are all as plainly visible through the glasses as the Bernina mountains from Muotta or the Bernese Oberland from Mürren. If you would have some idea of the whole landscape, go to Monte Generoso above Lugano. Look down thenec upon the vast plains of Lombardy and Piedmont and, instead of the Lakes, imagine at your feet large forests of dark cedars. Away in the distanee, as a background, place the chain of great peaks running from Monte Generoso to the Finsterhorn and Mont Blanc as far as the Col di Tenda. These will in a measure represent the mountains here: Nanda Devi, Badrinath, Kailas and Pir Panjal, with the peaks of Nun-Kun further on, rising above Zoji-là close to the blue plains of Kashmir. And how about distance? Well, Nanda Devi the abode of the gods and the roof of the world lies 150 miles away, Pir Panjal only 80, while the mountain I take to be Nanga Parbat, lying to the left of the twin peaks of Nun-Kun, may be something over 300 miles.

So pure, so unpolluted, is the air that to breathe it is sheer joy. And so we linger, revelling in the beauty of this land, acclaimed by many poets as the fairest land on earth, and follow with envious gazc the eagle as it wheels eircling overhead in the rays of thc sctting sun, till presently with the approach of twilight it rushes swooping to its eyrie. But wc envy none besides. Nay, are we not happicr than our fcllows? And so we turn and slowly make our way downhill through narrow gulleys and darkling woods and out again over the sun-scorched slopes, hastening to reach the camp lest the waning daylight leave us in the lurch.

CHAPTER III

DOWN TO THE SUTLEJ RIVER

NARKANDA lies 9000 feet, Rampur only 3000 feet, above the level of the sea. Now and then we both take a look into the deep valley of the river, and I can assure you it does not look at all inviting. At first the going is good. The way gradually descends the slopes of the hill, which are still clothed with cedar trees. Pheasants fly up and over the road. A troop of apes hoot at us from the safe vantage-ground of their tree-tops, while other apes, the brown baboons that live mostly on the ground, take to their legs, making all manner of grimaces. Through the trees we keep getting glimpses of the yellow fields below, until a few miles further on the woods suddenly cease and we emerge into the blazing sunshine.

The hillside is laid out in the usual way in slanting terraces. On most of them the corn is already cut—this in mid-July, mark you—and there are women dotted about, hard at work getting in the harvest. Before long we come within sight of the prosperous village of Kotgarh, which is specially famous as being the most northerly place possessing a Christian colony in this land of Hinduism. A little church lies nestling in the recesses of a cedar grove, and there are some rather pretty-looking houses. These are of two storeys and profusely decorated with wood-carving. The spacious balconies make a particularly pleasing impression, except when closed in up to the roof with

THE SUTLEJ JUST ABOVE RAMPUR
SHOWING ALTERNATE STRATA OF WHITE QUARTZITE AND GREEN HORNBLENDE

(Face p. 34.)

THE CAPPARIS (ROCK SHRUB)

wooden trellis-work forming the cages wherein the high-caste Hindu women are kept.

At this point the road dives sharply down and the landscape suddenly changes. We lose sight of the distant view and find ourselves in a gulley with walls quite 3000 feet high, greatly impeding our view of anything, especially as the valley keeps changing its direction every mile or so owing to the windings of the river. The mountainsides are so precipitous that cultivation is out of the question, for the rains of the monsoon swirl down and wash away every vestige of soil. But there are flowers growing in the crevices of the rocks: pinks, snap-dragons, sedums, and notably euphorbias (spurge). In fact the euphorbia, of the giant or tree variety, is the most characteristic feature of the landscape. Dry and of a yellowish green, it rears its countless naked branches to the sky and seems to cry aloud in protest at the heat and aridity of these hillsides. For it is now becoming really hot with a vengeance. The road too is bad, full of boulders, and so steep that one gets on better at a sort of jog-trot, than at a decent steady-going pace. But this springing and hopping, turning and twisting with the windings of the path, perpetually having to pull up short and always on the alert to avoid falling, is not only a fatiguing business but also a pretty hot one. Every stitch of clothing that can be spared is stuffed into the knapsack, which to Santoo's annoyance I generally carry myself so as to have the camera handy. The sun-helmet, however, one can't dispense with. From beneath its shade the sweat pours down the cheeks, and drips at every step from nose and chin upon the reflex-camera, which for convenience sake I carry strapped to the chest as entailing less risk to it when springing downhill. That evening, and almost every day we passed in the valley after that, I had to wipe this camera with a damp sponge to remove the crystallisation of sweat.

Higher up we heard the partridges calling among the corn. Here we have only pigeons. In the great euphorbias there are turtle-doves, while on the other side of the valley numberless pairs of rock-doves are seeking the cool shadow of the overhanging rocks. Before us and behind, beneath us and overhead, nothing but precipice with only a stone-strewn path. Down below is a gulley of steadily increasing depth, the river at the bottom being quite lost to sight. In the sky above nothing but a glare of blazing sunshine. That day we realised as never before, not even in the worst heat of the desert or of the Red Sea, why it is that our countrymen in the East Indies have special names of their own for our 'dear old sun,' the most euphonious of them being 'the brazen hussy.'

The heat in that valley was really past belief. Not a breath stirred to relieve the air on those bare declivities, where the temperature is above blood heat. As our blood has only a temperature of 98·4° and the heat here in the shade is 104° to 107°, sometimes as much as 113°, what it can be on the rocks I tremble to think! I was not able to register it myself but figures of 140° to 150° are frequently taken. Added to the heat of the sun there is the heat radiated by the rocks themselves: they are so hot that you cannot put your hand upon them. No wonder that you see the lizards and snakes literally shooting along the hillside, while the grass-hoppers keep up a chorus which is almost deafening at times.

All the time we are still continuing to descend, though the barometer we use for recording altitudes falls far too slowly to please us. Now and then the path changes to a rocky stairway with big irregular steps, and the going is by a series of jolts that gives one a throbbing in the head. At last we cateh a glimpse of the river, but at what a distance! We seem to have got no more than half way down, and so far as we can see the bottom of the ravine is quite as bare and desolate as the precipice along which our footpath goes. But there should be a fairly big village a little further on round the corner of that ridge, whither our winding path seems to lead. So we go on jolting and bumping down the hill. We have left the servants far behind on the stony hillside. They are not accustomed as we are to go at a jog-trot down the side of a hill, a thing only learnt by practice.

Suddenly the river is visible close below, but the last 600 feet or so are practically perpendicular, so that the path has to turn sideways along the slope and, after all this hazardous descent, actually starts going up again! But not for long, fortunately. Presently it stretches before us nearly level along the side of the hill, a long white streak in a wilderness of grey. The sun stands vertical in the heavens. There are no shadows in this landscape. The deathly silence is only broken by the alluring sound of rushing water from the river, as it flows far down and unattainable below. Thirst meanwhile is becoming a torment. We had made provision for this on starting, but what provision avails against such perspiration in so dry an atmosphere? Neither menthol nor even bananas bring relief. Liquid is the one thing needful. We press on towards the projecting ridge hoping to find some shadow on the further side, and possibly some water. Again the path rises, and our long stride is exchanged for a slow plodding up the hill. At length we reach the corner. The road gives a sharp turn and we enter a fresh ravine only to find the sun more fiercely grilling than ever. And not a drop of water coming down the hill. A bit of shade is afforded by a small projection of rock with some euphorbias growing on it. There even comes just a slight puff of air! And then—Water! I hear it bubbling out of the rock close at hand.

We scramble a little way down below the level of the path and reach the source. The water is rather dirty and turbid, but it cools the pulses and supplies refreshing moisture to our dripping brows. We take a real good splash and then sit down to await the arrival of the tea-pot which we have left far behind. Though late, it comes at last, and seldom has weak tea tasted so good; so good that it even gives us an appetite for food, and after absorbing nearly three quarts of it we all three stretch ourselves out comfortably in the small margin of shade. But the shade which was very small to begin with soon becomes even smaller, and at last too small to be endured. So we have to move. The sun which at noon was exactly above us, is by 1 o'clock shining directly under our rock! It has taken us five hours to make a descent of considerably less than 7000 feet, and we have another six miles before us. So we resume our march.

The path still winds down the side of the precipice, sometimes rising a little and then continuing on the level for a while at a height of some 300 feet above the river bed. I managed to scramble down to it once but only to discover more of the monotonous granite gneiss through which we had been walking for hours. I had not before realised its extent. On and on we go with throbbing brows and leaden footsteps. How long a mile can be! Now and then the path broadens out into a sort of terrace with a few mean huts about, and plots suggesting some attempt at cultivation. But everything is yellow, parched and sere. Occasionally we come across a wild figtree that provides us with some fruit and a bit of shade. The figs are only about the size of your thumb-nail but they are eatable anyway. Once, quite low down by the river, we came to an oasis. It was only a few paddy fields under water and newly sown. But the pale green of the sprouting blades gives a curiously fresh tint to the checkered fields with their intersecting hedges of bananas, all bearing unripe fruit despite their yellowed leaves. Hard by is Kepu, a place of rather bigger size than usual. Numbers of villagers and children lie listlessly about or seek oblivion of the heat in profound slumber under the shadow of a gigantic figtree.

Still on along the slope. I had sent on the mules by road to a point where highroad, footpath, and river meet, and a tributary as well. About 4 o'clock, after a march of nine hours in this awful heat, we pass a brook of deliciously fresh and clear water coming down in cascades, and our decision is quickly taken. We stretch ourselves out on the sand of the river in the shadow of a huge boulder. Santoo brews us another quart of tea, and Jittoo after a short rest starts off to fetch the mules, which by this time should be waiting for us further up the river.

The spot was an attractive one. There was a tall birch with a golden oriole's nest in it, and a flock of magpies were feasting in a wild figtree close at hand. But I had another reason for deciding to camp under the shadow of these trees. I had noticed that the rock formation had suddenly become black. There is an outcrop here of thick layers of carboniferous limestone in the grey granite on either side of the river. Moreover there is a bridge, one which by the way is as well worth a closer inspection, as are the limestone rocks in the dreary wastes of granite.

Oh, the bliss of having the tent up again after a day like this! But how about bedding? It is getting late, and apparently there is no straw to be had in the neighbourhood, so I order that our beds for to-night must just be laid on the ground. "Never!" exclaims Bier Singh the mule-driver. And up he scrambles along the hillside with the sickle he uses for cutting the mule's fodder, and within ten minutes we have two heaps of grass, bigger and softer than any truss of straw could ever be. One learns by experience, and it was nice to feel that our servant had himself taken the initiative in ministering to our needs. This kind of thing continued throughout our tour.

The next morning we are at the bridge betimes. We three propose going across to do a little exploring on the other side of the river, taking Santoo with us to carry the knapsack with the camera, compass, barometer, hammer, etc. But when I look round to see if he is there with his precious burden, lo and behold! all four servants are standing behind us, plus the two mule-drivers! And Jittoo is carrying the knapsack. What is the meaning of this? It is Santoo who always has to accompany us,

THE BRIDGE KEEPER

(*Face p.* 40.)

MEMSAHIB GOING ACROSS

because he acts as our interpreter, being the only one who understands English. However, he declares that he must go off in another direction to buy chickens and eggs and vegetables. It is a transparent lie, the fact being that he is afraid to come. Then I look at the coolie. Questions are superfluous. His face is quite yellow with fright. And as for our smiling Tara, he is actually shivering. Jittoo alone has preserved his equanimity. He nods and says in broken English: "Jittoo come Botsi."

But it wasn't so bad after all. The fact is that the bridge, a so-called rope-bridge or *jula*, did not look very reliable, neither was the bridgekeeper's wife, who was on duty this side of the river, a person exactly calculated to inspire you with confidence. However, we had already seen two or three people go over, and none had so far come to grief; so why should we? Santoo endeavoured to hold us back by saying that the bridge was only for the hill-people, not for Sahibs. But this Sahib was pig-headed and stuck to his point. So first of all our friend Traanberg went over. The sigh of relief from the servants when he got safely to the other side was a plain proof they were in earnest. Then over went Jittoo, full of bluff but looking a little pale for all that. My wife's turn came next, and I must own that I did then begin to feel some sympathy for Santoo. By this time he had turned, not as white as chalk of course, but a kind of cream colour. He held his hand to his mouth and kept shifting from one foot to the other. My wife did not wish to be lashed to her seat, and had no sympathy at all for the doctor from Rampur, who was on his way to visit a sick person beyond the river and had had himself bound with three ropes and blindfolded into the bargain. It is certainly a queer sensation. You sit in a double noose of cable-rope which is slung round a wooden reel made from a bit of cedar trunk, hollowed out so that it can slidc along the cable, or rather the combination of cables, that stretches across the river. Having settled yourself into the easiest sitting posture you can arrive at—there is no board, mind you—you raise your feet from the ground and shove off down the cable which hangs of course in a curve.

At first you speed along faster and faster ; then gradually the pace slackens till you come to a standstill, suspended over the very middle of the river, with ample opportunity of contemplating the rapid foaming current that tears along some fifty feet below. But beware of getting too much absorbed in your observations, bccause directly the cable begins hauling you across to the farther side it gives such a tug that you may be tumbled over backwards out of your uneasy seat. You next proceed slowly upward by a series of jerks, everybody lending a hand in pulling. Landing is no joke, for it is difficult to find a footing on the steep river bank. However, we all managed to get safcly over and back again, and after that the *jula*, or rope-bridge, had no further terrors for us, albeit the recollection cost Santoo some sleepless nights.

The stratum of carboniferous limestone, the black rock which had caught my eye, appears to be only of local extent, consisting of no more than a single fold about 160 feet high by 650 broad, measured from the river's edge. The riparian configuration is very different here, the sharp spinate formation of the crumbling limestone presenting a strong contrast to the walls of abraded granite through which we have been passing further up the river. And of course the vegetation shows a difference at once. For instance, in every damp and shady nook, the rocks are covered with the pretty maidenhair fern with delicate fronds and shining black stems, so familiar a favourite in our conservatories.

The next day we follow a bend in the river which brings us out on to the north-western slope. What a totally different prospect now meets our gaze! Here there is a dense shrubby jungle with an undergrowth of bamboo, the luxuriant tropical vegetation sustained by the water which trickles down the mountainside at every turn. There are hosts of birds everywhere: song-birds of many kinds, notably the bulbul. And there is the Indian sparrow, but with a most aggressive looking tuft set rather forward on his head. It is drab-coloured with the exception of the underside, which is glowing red or sulphur-yellow according to the species; both of which occur here. These birds are regular gamins, quite as noisy and talkative as our own sparrows. Sometimes there are splendid green paroquets screeching in the trees overhead, or there will be a flock of jays romping and clamouring like children just out of school. Everywhere there is life, a lilting, melodious, exuberant life. A contrast to the wilderness those few miles in our rear!

CHAPTER IV

THE STATE OF BASHAHR, AND ITS INHABITANTS

Our road now resumes its course along the bank of the river. At first the stream is sluggish, but as we advance the strength of the current increases, fretting its way ever deeper into alternate masses of hard rock and gravel and leaving a terrace on which numerous mounded divisions indicate the paddy fields that will appear with the coming of the monsoon. At present, however, it is all a howling wilderness. In the midst of this desolation lies the small village of Nirth, situated on the brink of a precipice with the Sutlej foaming beneath. I should call it a hamlet rather than a village, for it consists only of some half-dozen houses grouped round an open space down one long side of which are the temple buildings. In the centre is the Durbar hall. This is a mere wooden shed but decorated in the usual way with woodcarving. Hither comes the Rajah once a year to administer justice. But on whose behalf? There are no cases of theft except the theft of woman, and, as everyone knows, all is fair in love and war. The penalty for such misdemeanours is always decided by the votes of the neighbours, and is as a rule paid promptly. Neither are there any murders, because if you happen to kill anybody in a fit of temper or drunkenness, that is a misfortune, not a crime. One source of frequent squabbles is the right to land and crops. Water rights too are a special bone of contention, such as who

THE VALLEY OF THE SUTLEJ AT NIRTH

(Face p. 44.)

THE TEMPLE OF THE SUN AT NIRTH

may or may not tap the supplies of certain springs. Lucky mortals who are troubled neither with the existence of a legal code nor with lawyers! Here law is simply law, and swift at that. Whether it be always justice I hae ma doots. Anyhow, the Rajah rules supreme and everybody has to bow to his decree, no matter what it may be.

The temple reminds me very much of the temples one meets with in the plains. It has the same sugar-loaf tower that one so often sees in Bombay and Nasik, Delhi and Simla. But there are no horrible pictures of Shiva or Kali inside the building, only a solar disc with golden rays. For this temple, to all outward appearances so like any ordinary Hindu temple, is dedicated solely to the worship of the sun-god. Not the sun-god of the Vedas, the almighty Varuna, nor Brahma the Creator, often symbolised by the sun as the one elemental life-giving force; but Sureya the lesser sun-god of Brahmanism. Actually, however, the object of worship is just this same metal disc without any idea of divinity behind it. And as this method brings in most profit to the priests, the Brahmins are possibly guilty of instructing their disciples against their own superior light and knowledge. In the court of the temple we were struck by a profusion of oleanders in full bloom.

At Nirth we cross into Bashahr, one of the lesser states, which has preserved an almost complete independence. It is situated on the borders of Thibet, and the natives in the north-eastern part are principally Buddhists of a Mongolian type. Strictly speaking the state is considered as belonging to British India, though there is no distinct evidence of this along the road, unless absolute security may be counted as such. For since the British Raj has put a stop to the quarrels of the lesser states among themselves, or rather to the fighting-out of such quarrels by methods of violenee, peace and harmony prevail throughout the district, and the robber hordes, formerly sueh a menaee to travellers, have now disappeared. Not that regular highway robbery used to oeeur, but armed attaeks on peaceful villages by Gharwalis, Nepalis or the natives of Ladakh, often under no pretext whatever, were the order of the day. So that British rule really does stand for a guarantee of peaee. This, and a eontract with the Rajah for the eutting of timber in the splendid cedar forests, pretty well cover the sphere of British influenee here. The English are also responsible for the upkeep of the roads needed for tours of inspection, espeeially those used by the Forest Serviee, and dâk bungalows or rest-houses are provided at intervals for the officials who only oeeupy them for three or four days in the year. Otherwise the natives live on in precisely the same state of poverty as existed a thousand years ago, only deriving a miserable subsistenee from the produce of the ill-cultivated soil.

This remarkable state has a surface area of about four thousand square miles, *i.e.* rather more than one-half of Walcs. Of this, however, twenty per eent., or some seven hundred and fifty square miles, eonsist of glaciers and inaeeessible precipices with several mountain ridges over fifteen thousand feet high and so incapable of tillage. The lower levels are only valleys whose declivitous sides are mostly elothed with cedar woods. Cultivation therefore can only be earried on upon the terraees on either side of the river or in the actual bed of the streams. At the present moment rice is being planted in the lowest part of the valleys and above it some rye and wheat. But the chief item of cultivation is a sort of lentil with seeds the size of hemp. Millet also is grown and certain gramini-ferous grasses for which we have no corresponding name.

The natives live for the most part in small hamlets of anything from five to fifty inhabitants. Certain larger places have a population of some hundreds, and Rampur, the capital, has as many as twelve hundred inhabitants. The dwellings are not much more than cow-byres two storeys high, the cattle occupying the lower part and the owners living above them. Access to the upper part of these byres is obtained by means of a tree trunk with notches to facilitate climbing. Most of the houses stand against the side of the hill so that you walk straight off the beaten track on to the verandah which surrounds the whole upper storey. Here the men of the community, as well as the old folk, spend the greater part of the summer, under the overhanging eaves which afford protection from the vertical rays of the sun. In the autumn and winter, however, the eaves allow very little of the comforting warmth of the sunshine to be felt.

I have said "*men* and old people" advisedly, for the women folk do practically all the work. The only thing I saw being done fairly regularly by the men was the ploughing, which really is little more than addressing the oxen by means of a heavy cudgel. As for the rest of the work it is entirely in the hands of the women, who have to do everything, including the heaviest jobs. For instance, not only do they look after the cooking of the flour, but have to tend the vines which are used for making brandy, and see to the tobacco as well. For the Hindu is both a wine-bibber and a smoker, especially up here in the far north where the better principles of Hindu lore are set aside for the coarse customs of the hills. Other Hindu precepts, however, are eagerly adopted, for instance, the

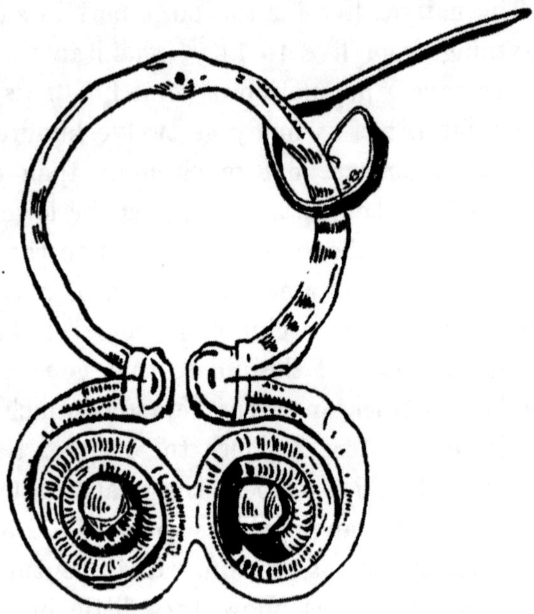

BREAST-PIN WITH PATTERN RESEMBLING THE HALLSTATT SPIRAL

economical plan of three or four brothers sharing one wife. But if so be that you have a very great deal of land to cultivate, well, then it is best and cheapest to have four, five or six wives, especially as theirs is in all probability the only available labour! It is indeed a queer country.

As we are on the subject of wives, I may here add a few words about the 'weaker' sex, who in this region seem more like men than the actual lords of creation. In fact,

INHABITANTS OF RAMPUR WITH THE WATER PIPE

(Face p. 48.)

HOUSE IN RAMPUR
THE FAMILY LIVE IN THE UPPER STOREY ABOVE THE BYRE

THE LOT OF THE WOMEN

the latter lead such a lordly existence that they make a pretty poor impression on outsiders. As everyone knows, the Hindus pride themselves on their Indo-European origin. Like ourselves they are Aryans. This in the higher castes is particularly noticeable in the features and the shape of the skull. But up here in the north the colour also of the skin is remarkable, being often as fair as ours, especially under the clothing. I never observed any instances of fair hair and blue eyes. In some parts of Kashmir these may occur. If so, Alexander the Great is responsible. . . .

The costume is very simple. Shapeless trousers and a long coat of woollen homespun are worn by the men, silver coins usually serving for buttons. The women's dress is a woollen shawl tied round the waist by a sash or a cord. One end of the shawl is drawn over the left shoulder and fastened on the breast by a clasp of a particularly interesting shape strongly resembling the Hallstatt spirals with which our own ancestors adorned themselves at a period when they too wore simple garments of homespun.

When we got to Rampur the place seemed half asleep, as a ten days' mourning was being observed for the Rajah's favourite wife, who had died a few days previously. This means that all the shops were shut and no one was allowed to shave or go about in white garments. The two latter orders were of course chiefly for the court. I cannot picture any of the hillmen in connection with such things as razors or white trousers. But it was rather unfortunate the shops should be closed. The backdoors, however, appeared to be always open ; but the stillness was deathlike. We were to return here later.

Our camp at Rampur was in a charming spot close to the river, which here foams thundering over some rapids. Being compelled by a slight indisposition to take things easy for a day or two I had ample opportunity of becoming acquainted with a certain peculiar rock-formation through which the river flows just here, and which we were often to meet with later in the side rivers, namely a pure white and very micaceous quartzite readily subject to cleavage and lamination. It is intercepted here and there by deposits of hornblende of so dark a green that, to the eye and in the camera, they show up as black in contrast with the white mica quartzite.

The flora here was a revelation to us. Both in and above the town are several hundred of agaves (aloes), gigantic plants with leaves over three feet long and flower-spikes measuring as much as thirteen to sixteen feet in height. One wonders how this native of the South American tropics has contrived to migrate to such an altitude in the Himalayas.

A less pleasant entertainment was provided for us in the shape of a thunderstorm with squalls of wind. Such a thing is common enough in our European Alps, but we had only once experienced it in the Himalayas. It gave us rather a *mauvais quart d'heure*, the rain pouring down in torrents, while violent gusts of wind tore screaming through the valley. Fortunately 'The Homestead' stood firm, except for the breaking of one bamboo tent pole which had to be supported by lashing a walking-stick to it.

Just beyond Rampur the road leaves the valley and we have to plod up the sun-drenched mountainside for some distance by a dreadfully steep path until we are engulfed in the cool shade of a cedar forest whose protection we enjoy till we get to Gaura. The following day we had two routes open to us. Either we must again go through one of the side valleys, or must go round it. We chose the latter alternative, and had a glorious walk by almost level paths with views of surpassing loveliness away to the snow-capped peaks of the Shrikan Dhar, a spur of the great Himalayan chain to which we were now drawing near. But the circuit was a long one and evening overtook us several miles from our goal, so that we had to pitch the tents hurriedly under a huge walnut tree on a patch of arable land. All went well until some squabbling magpies struck the branches, causing torrents of walnuts to descend upon the tents and, what was more, upon our heads. We could only be thankful they were not cocoanuts! The previous day we had camped under some apricot trees, and every gust of wind sent the fruit tumbling down into the tent. On that occasion we shot pigeons from the tent and with such success that they dropped straight into our kitchen.

The next day we had another adventure. We had chosen a pretty spot for the camp in a glade in the heart of the virgin forest. Around us were dense groves of ilexes and cedars and rhododendrons, and in the middle of the glade stood a clump of mighty chestnut trees. Gradually darkness comes on, the noisy clamour of voices is hushed, and the only sound that breaks the stillness is the friendly murmur of a mountain streamlet flowing close at hand. All at once there is a succession of wild yells in Hindustani, of which at first we can make nothing. Then we distinguish the word "Balu! Balu!"—a bear!

And Santoo comes rushing up calling to 'Baby Sahib' in broken English to bring his gun quickly, as there is a bear in a tree a little way behind the camp. He goes off courageously towards it with his repeating rifle charged with shot, calling to me to have my rifle ready. Naturally I can't charge the magazine as quickly as all that. Meanwhile there is a shot, followed by cries. Then more cries, and a sort of general scattering and finally peals of laughter!

What has happened? It seems that a short while before, one of the mule-drivers had left the camp to fetch some dead wood for the fire. Hearing a cracking in a cedar tree overhead he looked up and caught sight of a dark shadow in motion. At once he jumped to the conclusion that it must be a young bear and that the old one would not be far off. So back he went full tilt to the camp and shouted out a warning to us, with the result already described. Directly our friend Traanberg arrived he saw at once that the creature was far too small for a bear. A charge of shot brought the beast tumbling down head over heels. It turned another somersault as it rolled down the slope, and a second shot made us the proud possessor of a splendid—flying-squirrel! Tableau!

We came back in procession through the dark forest by the flickering light of burning cedar-boughs, and for some time afterwards could hear bursts of laughter rising from around the camp fire where our good fellows were preparing their simple meal.

The next day we are as usual early afoot. In the morning it is still cool, not to say cold. Later the heat of the sun becomes scorching. However, just now we suffer little from it as the road lies mainly along very steep cedar-clothed slopes. The nearer we approach to the high mountain chain the more the country above the woods takes on the character of a desert. We are now nearing Wangtu, the point at which our road crosses the river. Here we pass into the rainless district where the monsoon never comes. This makes it more difficult to find a good camping ground. All the mountain torrents are dry as a bone, and the only sign that they are ever otherwise is the bed of the river itself and the luxuriant vegetation. So we have to prolong our march. It is not agreeable, but it is impossible for man and beast to pass the night in a place without water. We are not made that way.

We strike some at noon, as about lunch-time our path returns to the northern slope. Here we find an ancient grove of cedars of a beauty and picturesqueness scarcely to be equalled even in this land of cedars. In the midst of the wood is an open space, and upon it stands a small temple whose pagoda style suggests Chinese influence. Here dwells a village god, an idol or *debthar*, similar to the *debthars* we are to meet with later. But he is withheld from our gaze. Neither money nor good words can induce the priests to grant us a sight of the sanctuary. For this god, fashioned by human hands, is so mighty that in troublous times the Rajah and his suite come hither to Paunda, as this hamlet is named, to ask his counsel and implore his blessing. So great is the value attached by the Hindus to this image.

Close to the temple two huge cedars had been felled. On their trunks I counted more than six hundred cones. Fire-wood for the Brahmins! It is high time that the

International Society for the Preservation of the Beauties of Nature made itself felt here; otherwise the whole of this lovely spot will be ruined by these vandals. I did what I could by pointing out to the priest that as every plant is a creation of the Most High it seemed to me such actions were calculated to bring down the wrath of the gods upon his head. I rather think my words made an impression upon him, and perhaps even more so the brand new silver rupee which I bestowed upon him by way of a peace-offering to the god. In return for this he kindly allowed us to admire the temple drums and trumpets.

We are now constantly meeting families of Thibetans. The young wife always comes first, a child at her breast and a heavy load on her back. She is followed by fifty or more splendid goats, long-haired and with prettily twisted horns. Each of the goats has two sacks sewn together and slung across its back. Then comes the old grandmother leading three children by the hand. Behind them another herd of goats, and last of all the father with the eldest boy, whistling shrilly to those that are lagging behind. In each of the flocks there are also a few sheep. A great number of these herds pass us, and we overtake still more. The latter are heavily laden with rice and sugar, while those coming towards us, in addition to the family requisites, carry salt and borax, the mineral products of Thibet. These people spend their whole lives travelling backwards and forwards to pasture their animals, going in winter to the valley of the Sutlej and in summer returning to their own country. But these roving herdsmen have become merchants as well as nomads and make use of their little animals, which only travel in the morning

TOWER OF THE SUN TEMPLE AT NIRTH

(*Face p.* 54.)

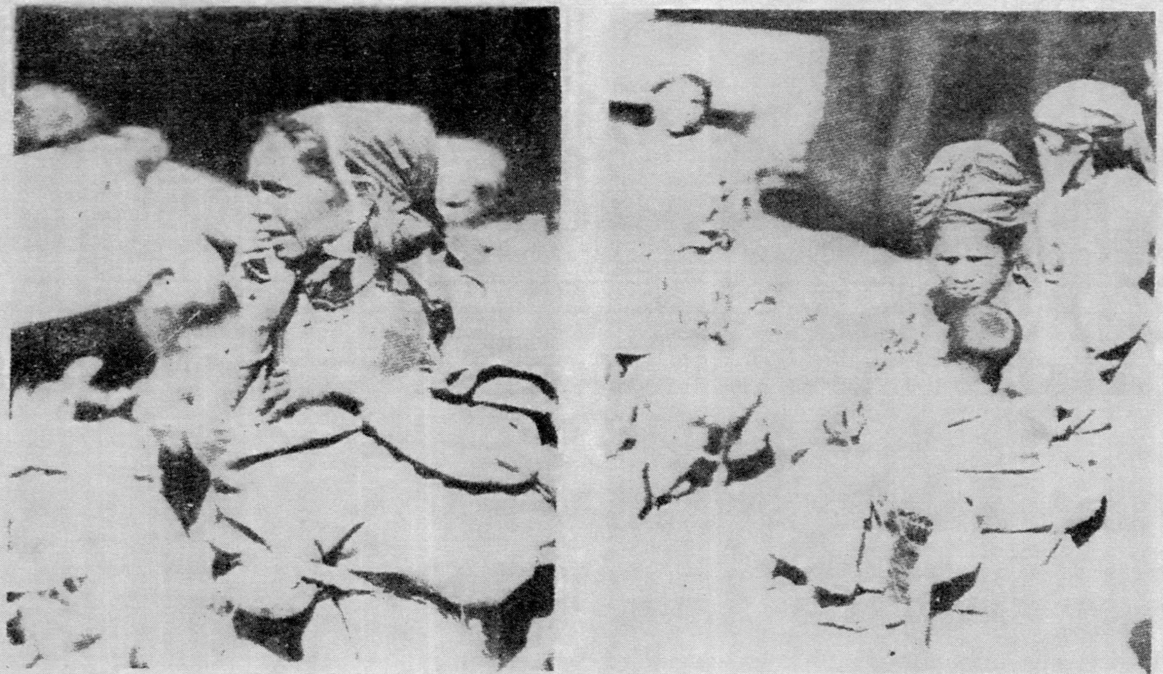

NATIVE TYPES

from four o'clock till about seven or eight and then graze, as beasts of burden. On two occasions we even met large herds of zebus (the humped Brahminy bull) all humping their packs in the familiar way.

These Thibetan nomads with their wives and children and animals are the principal travellers along this road.

A Kulu Shepherd's Bell and Tinder-Box with Flint and Steel

Their faces are all of the familiar flat Mongolian type but without the slanting eyes.

The natives further up country wear a most remarkable headdress: a sort of flat black pancake, decorated as a rule with something that has once been a coloured ribbon. And the funniest part of it is that the women's pigtails are tied on to the back of the hat with a bow, and generally no face is visible.

Later in the day we find all the herds resting by the roadside. The goats roam at will over the slopes while their packs are laid in a pile carefully covered with sail-cloth. Meanwhile the family takes shelter from the sun under a rugged tent full of holes, having lit a fire close by on three big stones and set an iron dish upon them on which they cook their cakes. These are made of meal, mixed with water in a copper pot or bowl. The dough is first kneaded by hand into a ball and then worked up by a series of dexterous twists into a flat cake. After the cake has been toasted for a minute or two it is turned, and finally is set up on end against the stones, allowing the flame to come close up along it thus causing it to puff out, and in a few minutes the *japati* is ready. Our servants eat five or six of such cakes every day for breakfast and supper, and these, in alternation with rice and *dall*, a kind of lentil meal, form their staple food. I told my wife she really must watch how it was done and try to make some, as the children and I might find them most useful on our summer camping expeditions.

There is not much incident along the road, but what one does come across is of interest. And the road itself is fascinating, going up hill and down dale, at one moment passing through the wildest mountain scenery imaginable, and in another five minutes through laughing cornfields or apricot orchards. Our *chuprasi*, the factotum lent us by the Rajah of Bashahr, always begins at once to gather the fruit. At one turn of the road we meet with a deer, and on another occasion it is a jackal. Frequently we come across traces of bears, and there are always lovely birds about.

Presently there is a tinkling of bells, of a lighter sound than mule bells, and there appears round a bend in the road a man who comes on at a jog-trot directly he spies us from afar. He is clothed in the brownish-grey native

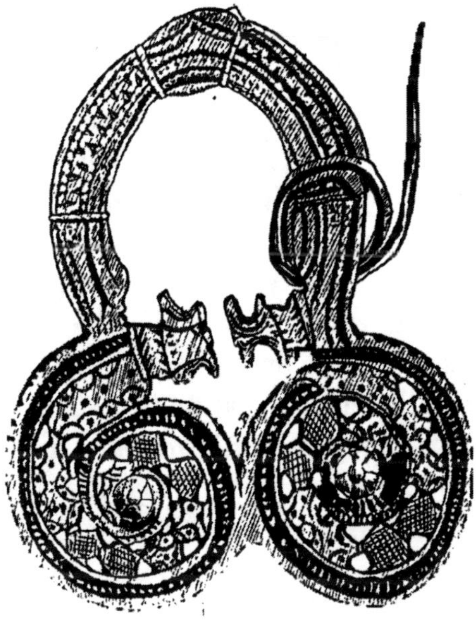

A Copper Breast-Pin of Handsome Design

homespun, which is more like our jute sacking than anything else. The natives weave it from the sheeps' wool and goats' hair of their own flocks. His upper garment is a kind of capote, and he wears trousers of Hindu pattern fitting closely to his skinny legs. He is barefoot and bareheaded with long black hair hanging down to his shoulders. A copper plate is tied with cord to his left arm bearing the words 'Mail-Runner,' or postman, and in his right hand he carries a spear with a bell on it; for as the post travels by night he might chance to meet with a bear or a leopard! The man, who appears to be a semi-savage, approaches us with a profound salaam and begins to undo a jute sack which he carries tied to his back. In another moment we catch sight of the pink paper of the *Hague Post*, and then out come several envelopes bearing the dear old Dutch stamps. How did he know they were for us, we ask? Well, he knew the Dr. Sahib was the only person who would have letters in an illegible hand, and so as he couldn't read the addresses he felt sure they must be for us. All this is conveyed by means of our interpreter, of course.

So our presence in the district is evidently beginning to be well known. The result is that people waylay us on the road or call at our camp in rapidly increasing numbers, asking us for medicines and medical advice. So much so that we generally have a separate fire going, around which the patients congregate until we have time and opportunity to pass them in review. A great many have ulcers on the legs and feet or on more delicate parts of their bodies, and there are many complaints of stomach and intestinal troubles. Most of the cases are infectious and there are also many of malaria as well as fever, the two being readily distinguishable. My excellent Santoo renders valuable assistance on these occasions, and after a few weeks no longer requires the doctor to tell him what to do for simple cases. He just asks for a little quinine or aspirin, and discourses learnedly on the virtues of *gurrum pani*, that is warm water, as if he had done nothing else all his life. He also knows that blindness and deafness are incurable, and that if a baby's eyes run it is a matter for the mother to attend to. Very soon he begins to noise abroad our medical knowledge and our supply of remedies, and many of the sick return the following morning with offerings in the shape of honey or milk, or a basket of nuts or a handful of apples.

And so we pursue our way. We are always meeting with something new, and every day is different from the day that went before. Life in short is really worth living.

CHAPTER V

FROM WANGTU BRIDGE TO CHINI KANDA

THE road continues its winding course, running fairly on the level along the mountain slopes. At one moment we are hanging almost perpendicularly above the Sutlej with a sheer drop of some 5600-6500 feet to the bed of the river. At the next we are making a detour of several miles in order to circumvent the deep ravine of one of the tributary streams. The river here has cut its way deep into the hills, and nearly all the valleys of the side rivers are what is known as ‘ hanging valleys,’ so that near the point where they debouch into the main river there is always a series of waterfalls and rapids. Only a few footpaths go down to the river, not more than one perhaps in the course of two or three days' journey, and they generally lead to nothing more than a few inhabited terraces. There are only three bridges between Rampur and Thibet. To one of these we are now making our way.

At Nachar there is an end to our lovely walks along the wooded hillsides or through fields of waving corn, for the road here dips into a gulley worn by the waters of the Sutlej through the hard granite rock, and the mountain scenery becomes bare and desolate. A rocky pathway leads precipitously downhill, sometimes by a series of zig-zags, while above the abyss burn the scorching rays of a pitiless sun. Hopping and jumping we get down to the bottom with all convenient speed, intent on reaching the

shade of the overhanging rocks on the further side of the river, and before long we arrive at the bridge. This recalls Tartarin's famous bridge between Tarascon and Beaucaire, being in fact *un pont si frêle* that no Hindu will cross it without an ejaculatory prayer.

Hard by, we halt and make ourselves a cup of tea, waiting for the greatest heat to pass ere resuming our march in the cool of the evening. Meanwhile we take the opportunity of examining our surroundings. At every turn one is struck by the enormous erosive force of the sand-laden water upon granite masses of an exceptionally hard nature, and one realises clearly how, at the period the mountains were upheaved, it was possible by rapid erosion for the river to remain in its old channel. The water flows in a brown turbid stream, tumbling along, gouging and grinding its way between steep walls of rock which, polished into the most curiously rounded shapes, rear themselves to a height of 30-40 feet above the surface of the stream.

The bridge is a wooden suspension bridge slung upon six heavy steel cables. It forms the connecting link between two districts which formerly were almost isolated from each other. Though four roads meet at this point, this crowded thoroughfare leads to nothing but a wilderness of rocks which soon end in a regular ravine where the crags tower up like steeples. Nothing but stone, stone, stone, as far as the eye can reach, the first thirty feet or so rounded and polished by the current as it cuts its way to an ever-increasing depth into the stubborn granite, while the upper portion of the rock-face is all angles and fissures, and in places crumbling away, a clear indication that the

formative process in these mountains has not yet ceased and that there is still life in the stone.

This I proved to my cost a little later on. I was sitting down quietly for an hour's work with my hammer, when in detaching some fine crystals from the granite I got a lump of falling stone the size of my fist right on my head, inflicting a severe wound. The result was that I had to take it easy for three days, so I had full opportunity of examining the rocks at my leisure. I should not have mentioned this little mishap had it not been the means of proving to us the spirit of helpful comradeship and mutual dependence that unites all civilised individuals in these remote places of the earth. My wife having promptly bound up the wound took the further not unnecessary precaution of getting me to bed at the Public Works Rest House close at hand, one of the buildings provided at intervals along the road for the convenience of travelling officials. I had received a most cordial permit to make use of any such rest-house in the event of our tents collapsing. It so happened that some coolies and other passers-by had noticed I was bleeding profusely, and accordingly, half an hour later, we had our first caller, a native student from Lahore who was camping in the vicinity. He came to place at our disposal his horse and servants to go for a doctor or render any other service we might require. By this time, however, I was sufficiently recovered from the shock to be able to assure him that I had all my wits about me and knew where I was, so that really I didn't need a doctor, but only required to rest for a while.

Three hours later arrives another Indian, this time the

Forest Ranger from Nachar, three and a half miles farther back on the road and some 2600 ft. higher than our present place of sojourn, bringing a pot of boracic ointment, a tube of aspirin and some roller-bandages. He had heard that a Sahib had been badly wounded and so had started off at once, bringing all the contents of his pharmacy with him, besides sending off an express messenger to fetch the Forest Doctor who was stationed fifteen miles further up. And the good man had to get home the same evening by lamplight; no joke mind you; for a matter of three and a half miles' distance and 2600 feet ascent means a good two and a half hours' climb!

The next morning a basket of vegetables and fruit arrived from a Forest official at Kilba, ten miles away, who sent a message with it to say that the doctor was at present visiting a sick native in the hills but would come on as quickly as possible. And come he did, at nearly midnight, after travelling twenty-five miles, the last ten of them on a horse belonging to the Forest official, a Mr. J——, the only European among the 100,000 Indians between Simla and the frontiers of Thibet. Mr. J——, he said, was coming himself the following morning. The doctor was a native and he had come without any antiseptics, so it was fortunate that he found everything going on well. . . .

Early next day there came a haunch of venison with Mr. J.'s compliments, and presently Mr. J. himself. He proved to be a nice young fellow who had travelled much, and we spent some pleasant hours in conversation. The outcome of his visit was that we moved the next day from this scene of rocky desolation to Sholtu, one of those

spots not marked on any existing map. Here the Forest Department has a splendid fruit and vegetable garden which Mr. J. placed entirely at our disposal. Starting off at an early hour in the morning we came, after a walk of six miles through a wilderness of primeval rock, to this oasis in the desert. At a place where the river widens, a terrace formerly covered by pine forest has been converted into a large orchard. This was a much more favourable spot than the one we had just left for a sick man's convalescence. Mr. J. came to see we had everything we wanted and actually went so far as to bring us a piece of Gouda cheese!

And so you always find it. However far you may have to go from centres of civilisation you will never lack help, for all people of education will stand by one another wherever they are. It is a fine thing to have this to rely on.

Meanwhile, I had found time to examine the neighbourhood of the Wangtu Bridge and the ravine beyond it as far as Sholtu through the glasses. Much of it is sheer precipice surmounted by shelving pastureland on so steep a gradient that a sheep or goat may easily start a boulder rolling like the one that broke my head. Everywhere the rock has crumbled away into channels and clefts, and evidence of former landslips is revealed by innumerable splits and fissures. In fact I was strongly impressed by the fact, confirmed at every turn by later observations, that this huge mountain-system is still alive, or rather that its active formative energy has not been quiescent for anything like so long a period as that of our Alps, for instance. And so as I lie there, three hundred feet from

the foaming river, my imagination travels away upstream towards the Shipki Pass and Thibet and to the Mansarovar Lakes and the remarkable controversy that has been going on in connection with them. The name of these sacred lakes, whence all India's holy rivers spring, has become widely familiar through the descriptions of Sven Hedin. But what is less generally known is the fact that the explorers who have visited these regions have brought back very conflicting accounts of the lakes and their effluents. One traveller unhesitatingly asserts that they are the source of the Sutlej, and describes the foaming torrent that issues from the western end of the largest lake. Another visitor to the spot twenty years later, an explorer of great eminence, declares that the lake has no outlet at all and that if it did overflow anywhere it would be in an easterly direction towards the Bramapootra.

How can such conflicting reports agree, one may ask? But surely the answer is simplicity itself. A slight upheaval of the soil on the western, or a corresponding subsidence on the eastern, side of the lake would be sufficient to account for any change and so save us the trouble of judging between the differing verdicts of two distinguished men. Thus does one solve the great geographical problems of Middle Asia from the depths of an easy chair! But before doing so you must feel sure in your bones that the mountains are still alive. And this not merely because some silly sheep has set stones rolling upon your head, but because of the earthquakes you have experienced and the observations you have made while clambering about among the fragments of fallen rock; and so on.

I would lie thus for hours in the orchard gazing about me. The whole place teemed with life. Birds galore, from the little flame-coloured fly-catchers to golden orioles, green pigeons and spotted woodpeckers. There were tits and thrushes too and all kinds of lesser song-birds; and daws and crows were not lacking. Besides these there were numbers of lizards, some innocuous snakes, and, needless to add, bees and butterflies and bumbledores and dragon-flies. Also any amount of beetles, and last, but by no means least, myriads of ordinary flies. All this was a fine chance for my wife and she made a large collection of spoils, including among other things a dragon-fly of a hitherto unnamed variety.

One day a fly had been plaguing me horribly. After a bit it ceased its attentions and settled for a moment on a stone, when out popped a big lizard and in an instant the fly disappeared. That lizard rose considerably in my estimation. Presently it came nearer, and after disposing of some apricot skins proceeded to demolish a large grass-hopper. Then it vanished behind the piled-up stones of a garden wall, leaving me to devote my attentions to a young 'white-eye,' a bird the size of a tit, which was being fed by each of the two parent birds in turn. All of a sudden the mailed head of my friendly lizard reappeared in perilous proximity to the little bird. Reaching with my left hand for the camera, I stretched out my right for my small rifle. Too late! With one dart the lizard seized the little bird and made off with it, while my shot fell harmlessly on the stones round his hole.

But that lizard was to meet with his deserts. The same afternoon, as he was lying stretched to his full fifteen

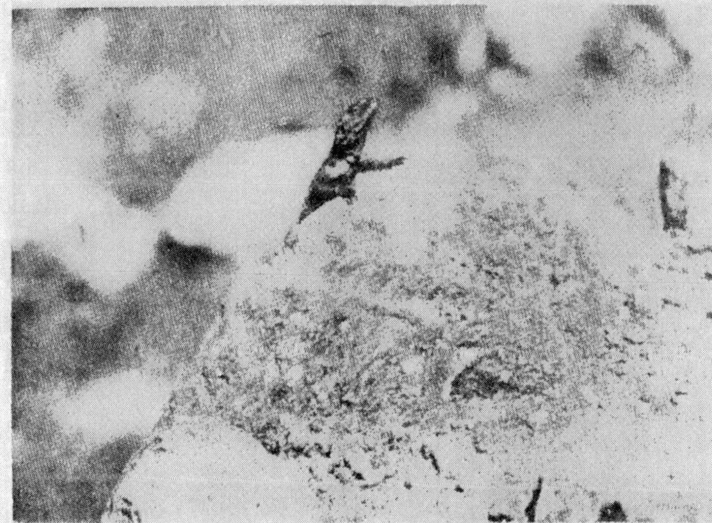

MY FRIEND THE LIZARD

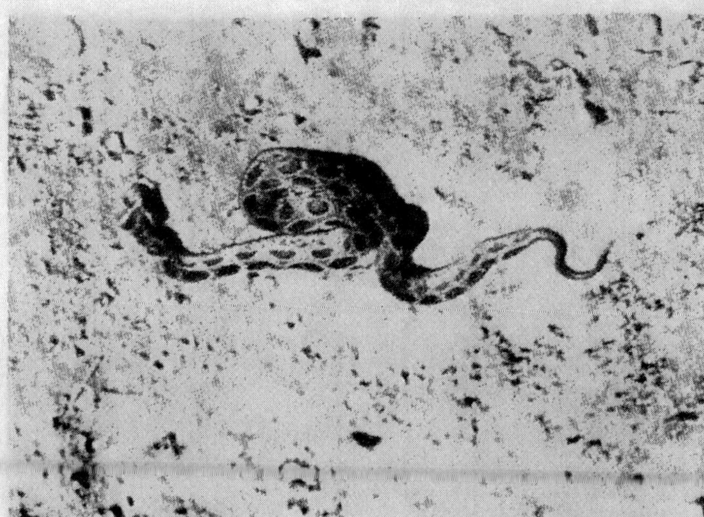

A SPECIES OF VIPER

(*Face p.* 66.)

A NATIVE PASSENGER

FERNS

inches in the sunshine, gorged and indolent after his juicy mouthful, suddenly, whence I know not, up came a snake, seized the lizard's head in its jaws, and before I could do anything, glided off with him into the depths of obscurity. I had not the luck to see the snake caught by an eagle and devoured in its turn, or the episode would have been complete.

Whilst I was thus doomed to idleness, and my wife was busy pickling reptiles, our friend Traanberg went a-shooting. I give the following extracts from his journal.

"This morning waked at four by Santoo, who had laid breakfast in front of the tent. The stars still shining. '*Goral* shoot!' cries Santoo, dancing with delight at being allowed to come with me. I carry the bear-gun; he has the knapsack and rifle. Presently he takes off his shoes, a sure sign that the road is getting difficult. We mount rapidly, cross the H.T. road, and then toil up a steep rocky incline consisting entirely of quartzite of so hard a nature that the nails are torn from my shoes and keep slipping out at every turn. But Santoo goes forward barefoot with that eternal smile of his. Soon we reach a small secluded 'nullah,' and a moment later I see something stir behind a rock. I cock my rifle and we go gingerly forward. All at once something gives a little spring and there, like a figure carved in oak, is a young buck *goral* standing among the crags about 400 feet above me. Bang! The rocks echo to a shot from my 10.75. There is a cloud of dust on the spot where 'the strength of the hills' has just stood, but nothing else visible. Can I have missed him? Up I climb to the spot where the big antelope was, and find him lying there in all his grandeur, dead as a door-nail, shot right through the back just above the shoulder-blade. Santoo capered for joy and got me to photograph him standing by the dead beast, afterwards carrying the full weight of it on his shoulder for an hour and a half, while I took charge of the knapsack and the two guns. *Goral* (the Himalayan goat-antelope) is excellent to eat, though this particular one was not so succulent as the gazelles of the Red Sea. The Hindus are very fond of *goral*, so—thanks to the bear-gun—the whole camp had a banquet."

After lingering for three days in Sholtu we resumed our journey. This entailed climbing from our present altitude of 6000 feet to Chini, which is at a level of 9000. You ascend by steep zig-zags, the path roughly hewn in precipitous masses of ocellate gneiss. This is a beautiful rock with veinings of green or black, interspersed with white spots about the size of a penny and often having brown dots on them. The large felspar crystals have been produced by the gradual cooling of the liquid rock. At some subsequent period another liquefaction has taken place, rounding off the angles of the crystals and thus giving the white spots their ocellate form.

The flora necessarily changes as we ascend. After Wangtu we find ourselves in a peculiar sort of desert climate. The snowfall in winter is considerable, but from March to October there is practically none. Thunderstorms scarcely ever occur and even rain showers are infrequent. The monsoon, which in the foothills turns the whole district into a kind of wet sponge, does not penetrate to the Himalayas proper, and while the great cloud-masses, striking the topmost peaks of the chain, discharge themselves over the foothills, Chini rarely has a summer day without sunshine. An ideal country for the tourist. The only drawback is its being too far away for a summer holiday.

From the foregoing it follows that the vegetation here depends entirely on the streams issuing from the glaciers and snowfields. Desolation prevails in those places which this water cannot reach, especially further up towards Thibet. Wherever snow water is available it is diffused through numerous irrigation channels over large areas, making it possible for whole villages to exist and flourish. In the valley there are scarcely any trees, but here on the slopes the pine reappears, notably a new species of it: the *Pinus gerardianus*, whose huge cones contain an edible seed. There are also of course the *Cedrus deodara*, and the *Pinus excelsa*, with long thin needles and still longer cones like those of the spruce-fir. These we find right up to the tree-limit.

We toil slowly up for more than 3000 feet by the usual zig-zag path, after which the way is fairly on the level along a grassy slope, becoming later steeper than ever, until we come out high above the Sutlej. Then a tramp of some miles in the valley of one of the side-rivers to avoid losing too much of the altitude we have gained. And finally we come to arable land and villages providing camping grounds, whence the pastures roll invitingly upwards towards the naked peaks above.

One of the peaks, a monster some 6000 feet high, rises just behind our camp, its last 3000 feet practically perpendicular. Towards evening, when the rocks began to cool after the scorching heat of a cloudless day, three avalanches of stone came down in succession, each consisting of dozens of blocks as big as a house. Great clouds of dust rose, filling the whole ravine, while hosts of smaller fragments rattled down after them. This sort of thing occurs daily. At the foot of the vertical slope is a moraine, and below it another thousand feet or so of grassland, the lower half alone providing safe pasturage. Eastward the sheer precipice, its lower portion of a bright brown rock with patches of yellow, falls away to sloping meadows. We rapidly make our plans for the morrow, which are to include a nearer inspection of these rocks, and for the rest of the evening amuse ourselves with watching half a dozen vultures with wings outspread chasing each other away from a dead mule.

Early next day we are afoot. That bit of pasture land proved awfully steep! Thousands of feet below in the Sutlej valley there would be short commons for a Dutch cow. And yet up here there are horses grazing, and asses and cattle, and of course goats and sheep. There are masses of thyme on the slope filling the air with fragrance, and a species of burnet ranging in colour from yellow through orange to the darkest shade of red. On the skirts of the wood little azaleas are in bloom. Blue redstarts with orange breasts flit hither and thither, and a tree pipit soars jubilant aloft fancying himself to be a lark. But at the height of some fifty feet he can rise no further and comes planing down to earth just as our larks do in the spring. A brook is flowing diagonally across the meadow, its margin yellow with marsh-marigolds. Funny to see them here in these strange surroundings so far from our own lovely meadows. As we approach the mountain

NEAR THE WANGTU BRIDGE
WATER EROSIONS IN THE GRANITE

CHINI KANDA
THE ARRIVAL OF THE MULES

(Face p. 70.)

THE TEMPLE AT PAUNDA

crest the barometer marks an altitude of 15,000 feet. Barometric pressure is barely 760 millimetres. No wonder that our breath comes faster and our legs go slower!

But we have a splendid rest when once we get to the ridge which runs up sharply behind us to the imposing height of 16,000 feet. One side of it is perpendicular. The other appears steep, it is true, but the ascent is gradual and clothed with verdure at least for the first three or four thousand feet. The sun is deliciously warm up here, the *japati* couldn't taste better, and when we wake after an hour's nap the horizon, which previously was veiled in a blue haze of night mist, has now become clear. To our right lies the valley of the Sutlej with Sholtu and Paunda and Sarahn, and in the background Narkanda and Mount Hattu. On our left is the steep descent to Rogi and the mountain ridge behind which Chini must lie. And that peak towering above it? The map gives it as Raldang, 20,000 feet high, and the beginning of the chain which extends opposite Chini, just as the Bernese Oberland extends opposite the Scheidegg.

A stiff climb brings us to the yellow rocks. It is as I thought: they are of grey granite gneiss covered all over with lichens, growing in the same orange and yellow patches and circles that we find on our own basalt slopes. They cover all the older fragments of rock and are the first signs of that encroachment which presently under the protective conditions of the atmosphere will make further plant life possible. Up here at tree-limit the lichens work in silence and yet they speak to us in clearest tones. "Here is safety," they say. "Here you may pitch your tents in peace. But yonder, where the lichens can find no foothold, where the weather-beaten crags are bald and cold and grey, is the rocky zone. And there every change of temperature spells danger to life and limb."

These are little things. But a knowledge of them is an indispensable part of every mountaineer's equipment, and death is but too often the penalty for carelessness about small matters of this kind.

We next go downhill to Rogi and then have to follow the road further in the direction of Chini than we intended, for the precipices are practically prependicular, and the next three miles of the way have been made almost entirely with the help of dynamite. We keep on turning corners. Three or four thousand feet down, the Sutlej foams through its ravine. Eighteen hundred feet up is the edge of the cliff covered with pine trees that in some inexplicable way have managed to root themselves deep into the rock, forcing away great blocks of it.

The road presently winds into a larger ravine about half a mile long by another half mile wide. There is no stream flowing through this valley. The cliffs at the back of it and on both sides stand up sheer and vertical, and the strata are not only folded but crumpled. It is not therefore surprising to find that in one place the road in the rock has completely fallen away for a distance of more than 700 feet. The whole of this gap is probably due to landslips. We scramble down some 180 feet over the débris and crawl along well under the cliff, keeping an anxious eye on the rocks overhead, while beneath us flows the Sutlej at a depth of some 5600 feet. How our mules ever contrived to get along here is a mystery to me.

However, according to the road-menders they did pass across the gap, the animals going first without their loads. The drivers and servants then carried the baggage themselves over this perilous place. In order to get a picture of this immense precipice I had to take five successive photographs, focussing the camera each time at a slightly higher level.

For another half-hour the road continues winding among the rocks of these Chini cliffs. And then all of a sudden an unexpected sight is disclosed. Right in front of us lies an open valley, its green cornfields running up the surrounding slopes in the form of an amphitheatre. In the centre of the basin thus formed is a cluster of houses, the village of Chini. A large black patch in front of it marks the arable land belonging to the community, which at the present moment is being ploughed by eight span of oxen yoked together. We were not prepared to find such a fine stretch of prosperous land in cultivation at an altitude of over 11,000 feet.

Our caravan was waiting for us at a delightful spot close to the Forest bungalow beneath some lofty cedars. Table and chairs, salad, onions and rhubarb from the Forester's garden, gooseberries and green peas from that of the Maharajah—the gifts literally poured in. There was even a fowl and a dozen eggs.

But we could not linger in this lovely spot, and on the very next morning, after carefully sorting the baggage and storing all superfluous items at the rest-house, the mules were sent off up the footpath to Chini Kanda. We intended to ascend as near to tree-limit as the animals could take us.

At some hundreds of yards from the camp the path passes between a tree on one side and a crag on the other. Here the first mule knocked the trunk it was carrying against the rock, forthwith divesting itself of the whole concern and trotting through without turning a hair. Number two did ditto, and so did mule number three. When it came to the fourth mule we thought it time to do the unloading ourselves. Three times was this performance repeated in the course of the first mile. Otherwise we got on better than we had anticipated. By this time there was no path at all, though probably it may have existed at one time. We knew pretty well, however, the general direction we had to take, having reconnoitred the previous evening. All the same we had once to bring the animals up by a circuitous route through the forest while we ourselves pushed our way uphill more expeditiously by dint of scrambling and clambering across the slanting meadows and rocky inclines. But it cost us a good six hours' work to get up 3000 feet. Once arrived, however, we found such a camping ground as I hope some day I may have the good fortune to revisit. This was a deep basin high up in an offshoot of the forest so that we were sheltered on every side from the blasts of wind which draw down from the glaciers at sunset and are the greatest foes to those who camp out. In the middle of the camp was a spring of water, crystal clear, and abundance of dead wood everywhere, a great boon at such an altitude and especially in the midst of a wilderness. The barometer now indicated an altitude of 15,375 feet, *i.e.* higher than the summit of the Jungfrau, and to the north-east we had a clear view of "The Great Himalaya."

Kailas, Jistingrung, Raldang. The names are barbaric and may be forgotten. But the panorama displayed before us during that week at sunset and sundown, veiled in evening mists or pellucid as glass under the rays of the noontide sun, was something infinitely grander, infinitely more beautiful than anything of which a photograph can give you an idea. Which does not, however, cause me to regret that our camera happened to be in good working order!

CHAPTER VI

CHINI KANDA

Our first night of camping at an altitude of 15,000 feet brought a certain disillusionment. We had purchased in Chini, by way of provender, a sheep, and had led it up with us intending to keep it for a few days and then use it for food should we run short of provisions. The very first night this creature attracted visitors to the camp. At about midnight the mules became restless and woke the drivers, who seized the opportunity to give a brisk poke to the smouldering fire. It was bright moonlight, and the great shadows of the pines fell across the camp sharply outlined against the intervening patches of radiance. And then just as the flames were beginning to die down again there was a movement somewhere in the darkness among the branches. One of the men caught up a brand from the fire and sent it hurtling through the air. And away trotted a disgruntled bear, highly offended by his reception. But we were not left in peace. Soon the mules cocked their ears in another direction. On the hillside above my tent were some low-growing willow clumps. Here too something was astir, but this time it was not anything black. Another volley of firebrands, and, with a great bound, out sprang a panther and went upon his way.

The men tossed a few more chunks of wood on to the fire and then crept back under their blankets. These fellows are used to the mountains and none of them would dream of waking the Sahib. But how he did let fly the next morning when he heard of these nocturnal visitors! My wife said she didn't know I had it in me. After that nothing would induce the worthy fellows to defer the slaughter of the sheep for one single hour. The creature, they declared, was a danger to the camp and—Well anyway, our interesting visitors didn't return and we just had to content ourselves with the mere sight of their footprints.

We devoted the next day to a thorough exploration of the vicinity, where there was much that was worth seeing. First of all, of course, the superb view which necessitated a constant use of our glasses. Up here it was not so hot but that one could lie at full length on a sun-warmed rock, and leaning on one's elbow, glasses in hand, could gaze for hours at the mountain giants before us and more especially at the colossal peak behind the camp that, rising at first by a gentle incline, at last soared up precipitously to a height of 16,500 feet. We were particularly interested in this peak and felt that the ascent of it ought not to be difficult, at any rate for the first two or three thousand feet. Further on one could not feel so sure about it. There seemed two ways by which we could get up to within a few hundred feet of the summit. But from where we now stood it looked as if those final hundreds might prove the last straw.

In the meantime, however, there is plenty to interest us nearer at hand. It is evident that bears and panthers haunt the neighbourhood, for we come across their footmarks and excrement at every turn, and the ground has in places been clawed up and bark gnawed off the trees

There are also musk-deer about in large numbers, and *goral* and other wild ruminants. And the district is rich in bird life. The forest literally swarms with tits and woodpeckers, goldfinches and canaries. There are heaps of pigeons too, which of course implies numerous birds of prey. Amongst the latter our buzzard. In addition to these there are, in the meadows above tree-level, many yellowhammers and birds of the sparrow tribe, besides blue redstarts. Higher up still we get surprises in the shape of redfinches. And the snow-partridge also deserves special mention. This pretty bird is a rarity and, moreover, delicious to eat. Beetles abound. In fact up to a level of 18,000-19,000 feet you never turn a stone without finding one.

Butterflies are less plentiful, consisting principally of a few azure blues, though there are flowers enough and to spare. Great masses of alpine roses, here of a creamy yellow, and a profusion of the little red azaleas. Thyme and burnet everywhere, and at the present moment irises and other plants of the lily tribe in full flower. The vegetation is of that rich order to which we are accustomed in Alpine valleys, only that it has less colour than the flora of our European mountains.

The rocks alone are rather disappointing. All existing literature on the subject, as well as instances of typically contactual phenomena down at Rogi, had made me expect to find distinct examples of sedimentary deposits here. But everywhere the granite still prevails. Splendid tourmalin crystals there are, and garnets; also some very pretty blue labradorite crystals, many of them several inches in length. But that is all.

Nevertheless it is a land rich in interest. So we decide to climb to a still higher level. Our intention is to ascend the slope just behind the camp and then, keeping to southward of the first snow, to try to reach the same ridge up which we had previously climbed to the height of 15,000 feet; but this time to get about 3500 feet higher. From thence we shall be better able to judge whether the crest of the mountain is accessible by ordinary pedestrians like ourselves.

Towards sunset we make for a point close above the camp where we have a free view of the landscape with Kailas in the foreground. Here we sit and watch the shadows of the hills at our back as they travel slowly upward along the vast slopes on the opposite side of the valley. Against the deep blue sky the whiteness of the snow detachés itself sharply, gradually changing from a soft rose-colour to a glowing red, until presently the shadow reaches the topmost peak and the whole long line of mountains suddenly stands out luminous and shimmering against a leaden sky wherein the first stars of evening faintly twinkle.

And as we linger we dream of that other Mount Kailas far away in Thibet, whose top soars high above the lakes of Mansarovar. There of old did the ancient gods abide, until the boundaries drawn 'twixt India and Thibet barred the way to faithful worshippers. The practical mind of the Hindu priests then hit upon the device of removing the gods to mountains more accessible, where the Brahmins would be better able to minister to the needs of poor pilgrims and take from them the burden of all earthly ills. And so it comes to pass at the present day Chini-

Kailas enjoys the distinction of being the dwelling-place of the most high gods. For how long shall these things be? *Tempora mutantur*, though perchance we shall not live to see the inevitable change—Meanwhile, Kashmir too has its Kailas; and Badrinath, the roof of the world, is another great rival, especially as the journey thither is said to be far less arduous than this journey to Chini. But what is easy is of little worth. In token whereof we mean to continue our ascent to-morrow.

. . . .

"Tea ready, Sahib!"

"All right, Santoo!"

I shiver as the flaps of the tent are opened. It is 4 a.m. and still pitch dark. But as we sit down on our heels by the fire, putting away a meal of porridge and fried eggs, the daylight comes quickly, both dawn and twilight being of short duration in these regions where the sun is vertical at noon and rises also vertically from the horizon

At 5.30 we are under way, and in another ten minutes or so have left the last trees behind us and are plodding up the grassy slopes in the direction of a great precipice rising sheer and inaccessible a good 3000-4000 feet higher up. You can't, however, see much of it as dark clouds hang about the summit. Lighter clouds like wads of cotton wool come drifting down the slope from time to time, enveloping us in a chill humid mist.

In less than an hour it clears somewhat. Below us in the valley floats a white sea of clouds, while an upper cloud-layer shrouds most of the mountain crest, only leaving visible the vast slopes up one of which we are slowly toiling. Presently the scene undergoes a sudden change. The clouds start a game of see-saw, now allowing a glimpse of a summit, then veiling it again; at one moment enveloping it as in a dank vaporous shroud, at another releasing it into glorious sunshine.

After first leaving the woods we had climbed up a stretch of meadowland where alpine roses everywhere encircled the slopes. Not the glowing red roses of our own Alps, but the tea-rose coloured variety. And, interspersed with these, there is more fragrant thyme, and single gentians, and campions like our Alpine ones only with smaller flowers. Primulas too, with the familiar spherical umbels, so dear to all our nursery-gardeners at home.

But soon there comes a change. Great patches of snow invade more and more of the hillside, and on the intervening spaces there is nothing growing save a modest campion or two. Luxuriant vegetation, however, has continued up to a level of 18,000 feet, the height of Mont Blanc!

Higher and higher we climb to the top of the great ridge on our way to the summit, taking a zig-zag course over the soppy ground, or cutting diagonally across the snow, into which we sometimes sink over our knees. On reaching the ridge we are brought to a standstill. The rocks have all at once piled themselves up at an impossible angle and there seems serious danger that, lying half loosened as they do, they may suddenly fall, like the avalanches of stones we saw the other day, dragging us with them into the abyss. The barometer registers over 19,000 feet, barometric pressure having gone down to 400 millimetres. It is a pity the crest of the mountain is inaccessible on this side, but ample compensation is provided by the magnificent panorama that is disclosed to view, one far beyond my powers of description. It takes in more than three-quarters of the horizon.

Behind us is the mighty mountain crest. On our right a bottomless chasm whence comes an upward urge of masses of white cloud. But soon the sun shines out in the blue overhead and in its warmth-giving rays all these white clouds crowding up the steep are swept away into nothingness. Occasionally between the clouds we cateh a glimpse of the Sutlej which, mind you, lies 15,000 feet below. And as the landscape clears we can see Urni and Sholtu and Sarahn and even Narkanda. Beyond it in the blue haze must be Simla. There is a clear view for a distance of more than a hundred miles.

Then we look to the opposite side of the valley. From the bed of the river the rocks rise perpendicularly. Above them are dense cedar forests with intervals of arable land in the broader parts of the valley and a few mean dwellings dotted about. Higher up is the tree-limit, and above that more steep pasture land, at this season deeply furrowed by streams of snow water, several of them still filled with the remains of avalanches. Higher up again are the rocky acclivities and glaeiers culminating in the loftiest peaks of all. Four or five of these giants rise before us each more than 26,000 feet high, *i.e.* over 7000 feet higher than the point at whieh we stand. You searecly ever see here any of those lovely glaciers on a gentle ineline. Nearly all of them are so-called 'hanging' glaciers, pitched at sueh an angle that avalanehes are coming down every moment. The roek-face everywhere is tremendously preeipitous, and there is something extraordinarily forbidding about the whole scene. In the Swiss and Austrian Tyrol many possibilities of ascent are always discoverable by anyone who keeps his eyes open. But here a climber seldom has a chance. An overhanging wall of rock threatening avalanches of ice at any moment, vast moraines at such a gradient that a single rolling stone may let loose a whole deluge of stones : these are the great difficulties that the tourist has to contend with in these regions. Added to which there is always the more prosaic drawback of 'want of breath.'

Yes, the scene is indeed forbidding. Forbidding, but how superbly grand! Menacing and yet alluring. Can one wonder that to the simple hillmen the farthest peak standing so remote, away there to the left, should be the dwelling place of his god? Kailas, the abode of Shiva, and of Parbati, Shiva's spouse. And the snow of Kailas is the vesture veiling the consort of the god.

As we stand there feasting our eyes upon this memorable scene, Santoo seated in the midst of his companions reads aloud from a little crumpled volume, translating from the Sanscrit for their benefit as he goes along. He is reading of the great bull that bears the whole terrestrial globe upon one of its horns, and how when he is weary he tosses it to the other horn. This is what white men call an earthquake. And the gods dwell high above the earth on the loftiest peaks, on Kailas and Badrinath. And Santoo craves the glasses that he and his comrades may gaze upon this mountain, the dwelling-place of god, and upon the snow which is Parbati's veil.

Far aloft, in a depression to the left of the summit, must stand the temple gleaming as gold in the rays of the setting sun. For hours a white wisp of cloud hovers relentless over that dip among the hills. And then—lo!—there is an exultant shout! The men bow their heads and fold their hands. The cloud has disappeared. And behold! a little rock, and upon it—the magnifying power of the Trieder glasses admits of no doubt—an immense oblong mass of rock at least a hundred feet high and tawny with lichen, as are so many of the rocks on these mountains. The famous Shiva temple of Kailas, built of devils and demons out of sheets of copper on a place inaccessible to man!

The eye travels further, this time to the north-east. That huge peak, steep and rugged as the Matterhorn and fully 28,100 feet high, is Pin Parjal near the Shipki Pass. It is only fifty miles away (Kailas is not even five). And beyond it is yet another giant. Northward again a whole chain of peaks.

The glass travels back again to the giant Parjal. This peak also plays a great part in Hindu legend. Beyond it at double the distance is another range of snow mountains. We consult map and compass. They are the Dog Mountains on the banks of the Indus quite 200 miles away in far Thibet. And a little further to the right, veiled in blue haze, lies the great plain with the Mansarovar lakes, those pools of mystery, the reputed source alike of the Sutlej and the Indus and the Ganges. Small wonder that we linger, dreaming in the glorious sunshine till the chill of evening breaking in upon our reverie compels us to beat a hasty retreat.

But we return wiser than we went. First of all we have discovered there is little chance of reaching the summit, but that probably on another ridge we may be able to get up some hundreds of feet higher than one can here. To do so we shall have to be up betimes. It has taken us seven hours to do to-day's climb of 3000-4000 feet, so laborious is the ascent in this rarefied air. Another thing we have learnt is that our servants are capital walkers. They don't suffer from shortness of breath nearly as much as we do, and they carry our knapsacks quite as easily up here as they do in the valley. But they are very poor-spirited. Nothing but the desire to get a good view of Kailas would ever have brought them so far with us. One of the mule-drivers who has done a great deal of hunting is plucky to the verge of recklessness when it comes to negotiating precipices. But as for the others! It is next to impossible to induce them to cross a snowfield, and they are ignorant of the most ordinary precautions necessary in passing over rough ground. On one occasion our good Jittoo caught sight of a squirming snake and hurled at it a stone as big as a cannon ball. The stone missing its aim came bounding down the slope with numbers of other stones in its train right on the top of us as we were walking along a zig-zag path some 1800 feet below. How on earth people born and bred in the mountains can indulge in such folly I can't imagine. But then it isn't easy to make a Hindu use his common sense about anything. In this case the theory seems to hold good that there are whole peoples and tribes entirely devoid of it.

After taking a day off in camp to cure the skins of the birds we had shot, dry our plants, write letters, etc., we start off on our new expedition up the mountain. Keeping this time in a more northerly direction we mount the hill at a fair speed, first crossing a large valley bounded on the right by high cliffs. The danger of falling stones necessitates our keeping as far away from these cliffs as possible until we reach an altitude of 18,000 feet, when they are replaced by a slope of turf. We have to decline the ascent of the first grass-slope as it shortly fetches up against another perpendicular cliff. But the second slope, as viewed from the highest point we attained two days ago, appears to be climbable. As we reach it the sun is just emerging from the clouds of night, for we have risen at cock-crow and made the first part of the march by moonlight. Coming along we watch the eastern sky gradually mantling in the light of dawn, the clouds hanging motionless over the great icefields till, the warmth of the sun causing a sudden rise in the temperature, they become the sport of the uprushing currents of air. It has been very delightful coming uphill in this leisurely fashion. But now begins the perilous part of the climb. We have to be tremendously particular that everyone keeps his place in the line so that none behind may be struck by stones set rolling by those in front. I have also to avoid taking steps too long for those who follow me. We toil on over the drenched pasture-land wet with the water from the melting snows, and then over walls of rock and little slopes of débris. Presently, as the sun suddenly blazes forth, we take a short rest, sheltering under a great block of rock from the stones that come tumbling about us every moment loosened by the warmth of the sun from the mountainside where they had been frozen fast. Then on again. Another difficult place in the rocks has to be traversed, then another snowfield and a final slope of débris, and at last we are on the ridge!

And what a prospect here unfolds before us! Again a world of stones and ice like that on the other side of the valley. The panorama includes five-sixths of the horizon, that is to say 300 degrees. The blocks of rugged rock of which the ridge is composed are so hot from the sun that the snow has melted away to within a foot or so of the edge. But down the slope to right and left the snowfield extends unbroken to the bottom of another valley where a pool of ice water has accumulated, dammed up by an outlying tongue of glacier. To warm ourselves, for it is chilly at this height, we roll great boulders to the edge of the snow and send them spinning down the slope into the pool, some hundreds of feet below, causing the water to splash high into the air. This incidentally supplies a proof that we can't possibly attempt descending here. Nor can we go any higher. The rocky ridge is tremendously friable, and only a small portion of it farther up is free of snow, while the gradient of the snowfield itself is pitched at such an angle as to present few attractions to anyone not contemplating suicide. The barometer registers an altitude of 20,200 feet. But there are still ranunculuses and saxifrages growing among the rocks, and as the heat of the sun steadily increases it is beautiful to watch the morning cloud-mists gradually wreathing themselves about the summits of the peaks and melting away into thin air. So we have not come hither in vain. There is plenty to see and enjoy.

For hours we linger there looking out over Spiti and Ladakh and Thibet. On the way back we give spirited pursuit to some more snow-partridges, and taking a short cut over the grass by a break-neck descent, manage to reach the camp an hour or two earlier than we expected, another day of pure enjoyment behind us. Round the fire that evening we hammer out the next part of our programme. We decide first to push on further to the north-east and make an attempt to reach the limits of the granite zone. Should this prove too lengthy an undertaking, we will cross the river and pay a visit to Kailas. The holy mountain lies behind the shoulder of a densely wooded hill which runs out into a kind of rocky ridge upon which we shall doubtless again be able to reach an altitude of 18,000 feet. We want to find out whether the rock-formation from the Sutlej valley, 3000-4000 feet above sea-level (of Amsterdam) up to nearly 19,000 feet on the shoulder of Kailas, is really, as we suppose, all of the same granite-gneiss.

The descent from our high-level camp was accomplished fortunately without damage to mules, etc., in spite of a damp day with drizzling rain at intervals which made the stones dangerously slippery.

CHAPTER VII

THE DANCE OF THE GODS

Scarcely have we descended from the higher spheres, in other words returned to our pleasant quarters at the Chini Forest Bungalow, when the 'mate' of the village comes in to tell us that a sacrificial feast is to be held on the morrow at a place a mile further on. The fields in the district have all been ploughed and sown; but the usual method of irrigation, namely conducting cold snow water over the surface of the soil at night and letting it stand all day to absorb warmth in the sun, is not exactly calculated to induce a rapid germination of seed. Rain therefore is much needed, and it is for the purpose of invoking this blessing of the gods that the said festival has been organised. It is known as a feast of sacrifice because a propitiatory offering of sheep and goats will be one of its chief features.

The 'mate' is a kind of mayor or burgomaster, whose business it is to provide such coolies as are needed, to ordain who is to supply strangers with chickens, etc., and to deal with various other equally weighty matters. On this occasion he is to act as our guide.

On the following morning, accordingly, we followed this worthy up a stony path along the hillside. My entire staff had turned out in its Sunday togs with snow-white trousers and turbans. Santoo had painted on all foreheads a red spot, the caste mark of the Hindus, using for the purpose some of the pear-juice taken out of the stores for our pudding. On his own forehead, however, he had drawn a broad vertical red line, presumably to indicate that he was boss of the show.

We started by cutting diagonally through a magnificent cedar wood, the kind of place where our forefathers might have had their altars, and made for a plot of ground in the middle of which was a small shed or pent-house. Inside it were three models made of clay, two painted white and the third red, symbolising the mountains whence the sacred rivers have their source. These were surrounded by numbers of other little clay mountains in the shape of sugar-loaves about two and a half inches high, placed here as votive offerings by the faithful. Each one was of course carefully orientated in the direction of Kailas, the giant mountain on the other side of the valley which I have already described as the abode of the most high god and of his consort.

A motley company had here assembled. Not a vestige of Sunday clothes in their case, the garments all being of a brownish-grey woollen sacking; but the men wore a bunch of flowers on their head-dress. This latter was either a sort of smoking-cap, resembling that worn by old men in Europe, only made of this same brownish-grey material and faced on one side with red, or else the flat Thibetan hat of black felt with an upturned brim. The 'mate' had a hat of this description and we dubbed him 'my lord Pancake' on the strength of it. This 'pancake' of his, by the way, was adorned with a piece of sterilised gauze with marks of blood at regular intervals all the way along it!

The ladies had bestowed a little more trouble on their

WAITING FOR THE SACRIFICE

THE GODS ARRIVE PRECEDED BY MUSIC

(*Face p. 90.*)

THE FIRST VICTIM

THE LIBATIONS

toilet. They also wore head-dresses of either the cap or pancake order decorated with flowers, the latter shape being most affected by the flat Thibetan, or Ladah-Chinese, type of face. Their ear-rings were as big as bracelets and they had ten of them in each ear. In addition they wore gold or silver nose-buttons and bead necklaces of red porcelain and green turquoise with silver pendants. The finishing touch was the outer shawl, in many cases embroidered with a pretty coloured design, but with a border of swastikas or Greek key pattern carried out, alas, in coloured wool imported from Germany! I only saw one damsel with ornaments exclusively of gold and with a white shawl and head-dress. Needless to say one woman out of every three had a child on her back. The most noticeable thing about the whole crowd was that they had all washed themselves.

The company was picturesquely grouped round a dozen wood fires upon which *japati* and soup were in process of cooking. Sheep and goats were tethered here and there. We lit another fire for ourselves and sought out the softest stones we could find to sit upon. The cook on going to fetch another stone for his kitchen discovered underneath it three scorpions as long as my finger. The place was literally swarming with these ugly customers, so we migrated to a huge block of rock.

Presently there is a blare of trumpets accompanied by a roll of drums and everyone hastens to the dancing-place in front of the little temple, whence a singular procession is perceived coming up the hill. A big drum leads the way followed by two small ones greatly differing in tone. Then come two men with curved S-shaped trumpets about six feet long that give forth a horribly nasal twang. These in their turn are followed by men carrying copper plates and cymbals to the accompaniment of triangles. Behind them again comes another pair of gigantic trumpets twenty-five inches across. These trumpets are made like the former of brightly polished silver, and they give out the same nasal blare lamentably suggestive of a cannibal orgy.

Onward comes the music in a steady rhythm with a perpetually recurrent strophe, till at last the players reach a terrace immediately below us, where they take up their stand. And now there arrive upon the scene three enigmatical-looking objects which Mr. D., a Forest official present, introduces to our notice as 'native gods' or gods of the locality. They have been brought hither by their worshippers from three of the neighbouring villages that they may taste of the sacrifices amid music and dancing.

Picture to yourself a kind of old-fashioned shako such as was formerly worn by Cossacks—a huge shock of hair measuring three and a quarter feet in diameter and as much in height. Below it a gleaming circle of grinning masks made of gold and silver, cunningly embossed and engraved to simulate human features, with jewelled eyes. There are from eight to twelve of these faces around each god, all artistically wrought and adorned with semi-precious stones. The whole concern rests upon a square stool with bamboo poles stuck through it, one on each side, enabling the entire weight of the monster to be carried by two men. The under framework is concealed by pieces of silk in gaudy shades of yellow, red and green.

THE GODS OF KANGI AND TELINGI

(*Face p.* 92.)

A STIFF PULL

So these are the *debthars* or native gods about which one has read so often, but of which hitherto I had not even seen a picture. And now here they are, actually posing right in front of my camera! The high priest whispers to D. that nothing will come of it because the power of the god will be sure to spoil the plate. However, D. himself is a Hindu of old Brahmin stock and therefore of higher priestly rank than any others present, which indeed is the only reason why we are permitted to assist at the festival.

Meanwhile all manner of utensils have been brought up the hill. Dishes, silver pitchers full of wine, cloths, a pair of great grisly-looking choppers with silver mounted hilts, drums and trumpets, etc. The *debthars* having received a final rub, and the silver handles of their litters, which are also adorned with semi-precious stones, one more polish, everything is now ready for the sacrificial dance.

When the procession once more sets itself in motion towards the temple, the number of spectators has increased to a good three hundred or more. The women sit or stand in long rows round the edge of the terrace, where we also find places. Every avenue of approach to the festival ground is thronged by the men, all of whom have sheep and goats with them, the animals unaccustomed to such a crowd tugging to get free. The only unoccupied space is the terrace itself in front of the shed-temple, and thither the gods are now borne to the accompaniment of music. It is hard work. The bearers toil and lean on their companions for support; for the last pull is a steep pull, and when once they are up, there is no time to take breath. At this point the gods salute one another slightly

—that is to say, the bearers bring them close together and, holding them on a slant, make them bow, as it were. Then off they go round the square, the bearers jumping them up and down on the swishing bamboo poles, making them bow whenever they approach one another. And all the while there goes on a roll of drums and a series of wailing "ti-oo-oos" from the trumpets.

As soon as the gods have by these means been worked into a good humour, a halt is made exactly opposite us and a magnificent ram is dragged to the fore. While one assistant holds him fast another raises a chopper over three feet long with both hands. Whiz! it goes through the air, severing the ram's head at a blow, and the body, still kicking, rolls down into the gangway. Ere I have time to recover from the shock, a beautiful he-goat has also departed this life as well as two sheep; then one nanny-goat, and then another. A priest pours wine from the silver pitchers over the heads that are left lying on the terrace. Six victims have now fallen. Then the executioner—I should say the sacrificing priest—stays his hand awhile. But the music strikes up more loudly than ever and the procession moves on until the head of it is turned to the right, facing in a westerly direction. The bearers proceed by a succession of jumps which causes the monster divinities to start dancing again and bowing to one another as they sway to and fro. And the cold metal masks look down upon successive heaps of twitching carcases as each turn in the dance brings them to another point of the compass, until they are presently facing us once more. Fast and faster falls the knife. Men crowd one another aside in their eagerness to offer animals for sacrifice. Children help drag forward the little recalcitrant creatures, and watch with big terrified eyes the last struggles of their playmates. The smell of blood and wine mingles with that of perspiring bodies. Quiek and ever quicker moves the rhythm of the dance in a never-ceasing measure, while the sacrifices go on. You become aware that a religious mania is taking possession of these semi-savages. And, remember, it is only a decade or so ago that this knife was falling in self-same fashion upon the children of men. Nay, actually a short three weeks ago a human sacrifice, *sùb rosâ* of course, took place in Calcutta itself, the victim having first formerly declared his personal desire to be offered up to Kali the goddess of death.

On and on dances the mad hurly-burly. Between sixty and seventy carcases are now lying round in convulsions. The smell of blood makes me almost ill, and I withdraw from the front row where the spectators are still staring with rapt attention at the performance as though hypnotised, and stand at the back.

All of a sudden the raucous music stops. But the stillness is even more unnerving than the infernal hubbub that went before. And suddenly a weird idea flashes into my mind. What if some one of these frenzied and fanatic devotees should cry aloud that the god is angry, that he is about to send calamity upon the land, and that a special sacrifice must needs be offered to assuage his wrath ? In that case we are irrevocably lost. We are the only Europeans within a radius of a hundred miles. And we stand facing the holy mountain which all day long has veiled itself in clouds as though it had no pleasure in the strange spectacle enacted here.

But not a voice is raised. The gods are deposited under the pent-house, and the musicians draw aside and begin a new and calmer melody.

A young goat is now led into the arena and decapitated. But this time the high priest takes the head in his hands and begins chanting a prayer to the gods. He then dips his finger in the blood and on the foreheads of the gold and silver masks he makes a little mark similar to that which was imprinted on my servants' foreheads this morning. This, in former times, used of course to be done with the blood of the last human victim. After this, women advance with garlands to decorate the gods. Others sprinkle them with wine. Finally, with a waving of great plumes, made from the hair of the rare white yak, the ceremony is brought to an end. The spectators gather around the fires in groups according to their villages or tribes, while the bodies sacrificed to the gods are roasted to provide a banquet for men. For a few pence I managed to secure the heads of the first two victims of the sacrificial knife: a large ram and a he-goat. A fine addition to my collection of skulls.

More dancing was to follow, first the men going round together in circles and then the women, in time to the music. But we were longing for a breath of fresh air and to get away from the smell of roasted flesh, so we walked back to the camp, full of dust and new impressions. One could not help thinking of Phineas Fogg and the temple of Juggernaut in Jules Verne's *Around the World in Eighty Days*.

But if we had had enough of the festival, not so our servants. They were very anxious to stay on and dance,

THE HIGH PRIEST LIFTS UP HIS VOICE

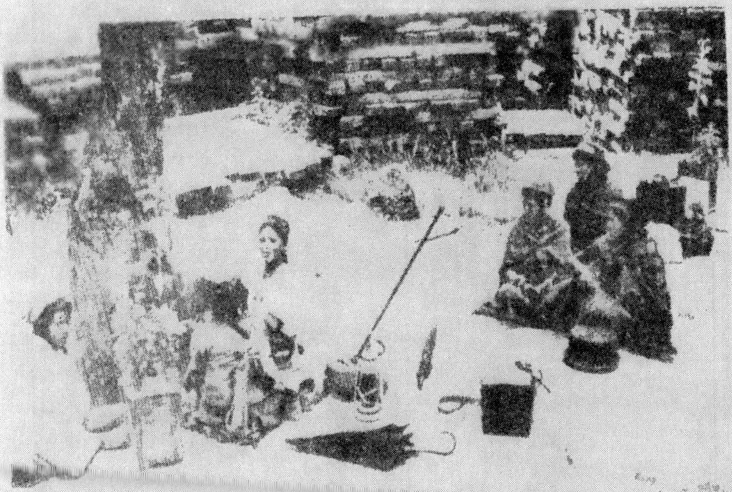

THE LAST COOLIES

(Face p. 96.)

KAILAS FROM AN ALTITUDE OF NEARLY 19,000 FEET

but naturally dared not ask to do so. However, the difficulty was solved by D. inviting us to dinner, which enabled them to remain behind without compunction. We first went back to camp to tidy ourselves up a bit and then proceeded to the Forest Rest House, where we spent an hour walking in the garden in conversation with our host. Then dinner made its appearance, and with it, to our amazement, our own men Santoo and Jittoo! They had come back to see that we had a good dinner!

And it certainly *was* good. First some julienne, then a dish of salmon and rice, and after that corned beef with potatoes and apricots. This was really one feast on top of another to us who had subsisted for weeks on pigeons and partridges or tough fowls and mutton. So at the end we thanked our host profusely for the warmth of his hospitality and all his kind attentions, and took our leave. On the way back I asked Santoo again why he had returned, and then the truth came out! He had been afraid that his Sahib and beloved Mem-Sahib would not get the proper sort of food nor enough to eat, our friend D. being a Hindu. It proved to be just as he expected. There wasn't anything in the place except a little rice, some nasty brown sugar and a few mouldy vegetables. He at once ran back to the camp and brought back one tin of salmon and another of corned beef and some apricots. There were enough greens in the garden to make soup. Meanwhile Jittoo had cleared the whole lot of dirty servants out of the kitchen, the cook included, and had turned to and cooked us this exquisite meal. So we actually had been entertained on our own emergency rations, which we had been at such pains to preserve! And the best part of it was that our friend the Forester had not apparently thought it necessary to enlighten us.

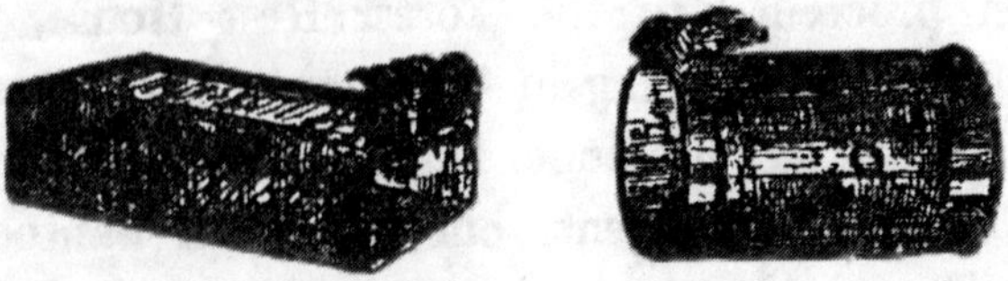

CHAPTER VIII

TO THE SHOULDER OF KAILAS

THE next day we moved on in the direction of the Thibetan frontier. D. accompanied us. He got my wife to instruct him in the pronunciation of French, which he murdered atrociously. This beguiled the way as far as he was concerned, for he had no eye for the beauties of nature. When we stopped for tea out came a pack of cards. We put two trunks together and calmly sat down in the middle of the road to play a game of bridge. No one could get by, so anybody who came along just had to sit and wait patiently till we had done. By that time there were five or six women on either side of us.

Mr. D. was a curious type of man. A Brahmin by birth, he had received a partly European education and had studied at the Forestry School in Lahore. A couple of years ago his father had wired for him to leave his studies and return home to be married to a woman he had never seen, the usual custom in native circles. Divorces and unsuccessful marriages are things unknown, for there is no question of your choosing for yourself. You are just set down alongside one another and you must both make the best of it. And so, for example, here is this young man who thinks he is living like a European and who smokes and drinks brandy and eats meat at the same table even with Christians like ourselves; a man who prides himself among Hindus upon his Brahmin descent and treats all lower castes as his subordinates—allowing himself to be married according to a code against which our own daughters have rebelled long ago. He is now learning French because his heart's desire, like that of all Indians, is to visit Europe, and especially Paris.

The road sweeps on in a great semi-circle around the projecting shoulder of Kailas which I have already described. The further we go, the scantier become the trees, and the parched air of the wilderness makes itself increasingly felt. By the time we reach Pangi and Jangi our surroundings are more like wooded steepes than actual forests. The width of the road contracts at every moment. In places there is only just room for the laden mules to scrape through. What really causes us increasing uneasiness are the little walls along the roadside, which are not built as a protective parapet but have gradually piled themselves up out of stones which have fallen upon the road and which cannot be flung further downhill without danger to other people. The whole landscape is rugged, steep and wild. So are the natives.

It is an extraordinary country. Pangi and Jangi lie at only ten miles' distance from one another and on the same side of the river and on the same highroad. And yet each village has its own language and the natives of

"OM MANE PADME HUM" IN TANKRI CHARACTERS
KAILAS IN THE BACKGROUND

(*Face p.* 100.)

TESHOO LAMA, A THIBETAN PRIEST

one don't understand the language of the other. The 'mate' of the village is the one man who knows Hindustani, the recognised language of the northern part of British India. However, you can get on wonderfully well by means of signs, which you learn fast enough by intercourse with these simple folk who are only too anxious to understand you. Pangi is the furthest point to which Europeans as a rule penetrate. Most of those who come hither are Forest officials. The dâk bungalow was built for the first of these men. It was he who adopted the goodly custom of cutting his name on the oak table, and this interesting article of furniture now recalls the names of all the Europeans who have visited the spot during the last fifty years. We followed their examples, on the chance of one day seeing our names exhibited with the rest in the British Museum!

Everything now indicates that we are approaching the confines of Thibet. All along the road we come across the work of Buddhist priests and mendicant friars, in the shape of great stone benches, some no less than 300 feet long by over 3 feet wide. Upon them are set up large numbers of boulders, or rather stone slabs, with beautiful Tankri characters scratched upon them. Once our attention was arrested by the intaglio of a lotus flower. In most cases, however, there is nothing but an endlessly reiterated series of the formula: "*Omne mane padme hom,*" which roughly translated is: "O eternal praise of the lotus flower."

Once or twice we meet priests of the slit-eyed Mongolian type who look askance at everybody with an air of timidity and suspicion. The priest here represented is a favourable exception. He actually allowed us to interview him in broken Hindustani, and told us that in obedience to the precepts of Buddha he had spent twenty-five years of his early life in study, had then lived his life in the world for another twenty-five years, and subsequently on his fiftieth birthday had left house and home, wife and children, to take his turn in spreading the doctrines of the Buddha and following in his footsteps. These duties were now taking him down to the plains. All the time he kept up a ceaseless muttering, passing the beads of his rosary through his skinny fingers. And the burden of his song was always the same: "*Omne mane padme hom.*" When I asked him what it meant he gave the translation above-mentioned, but to my further question, why the lotus flower should be so extolled, he vouchsafed no reply. I approached the subject in various ways and at last became convinced that this Lama priest was totally ignorant of the fact that the lotus blossom is the symbol of the dawn, from which the sun, the emblem of Brahma, is born anew each morning. One is struck afresh, every time one comes into contact with Buddhists in these regions, by the elaborate ritual, the slavish obedience to the commands of the priests, the endless vain repetitions of mere senseless words, and the entire absence of any trace of the beautiful thoughts which Westerners profess to discover in the Buddhist faith.

The road from Chini at first runs fairly level at an elevation of about 15,000 feet until, close to the Shipki Pass, it runs up to an altitude of almost 26,000 feet where we enter the treeless region of Thibet. We had taken leave of Mr. D. and were now descending into the valley to seek a suitable place for crossing the river. The current here is exceptionally strong, so that we were lucky in finding the Rope Bridge in excellent condition. It was moreover of quite modern construction, having been renewed by the Forest Department when the old one recently gave way. A stout steel cable unites both banks of the stream, and the little seat has quite a nice board to sit upon. It is suspended by a double pulley running over the steel wire—a great improvement on the old-fashioned method. This time Santoo thought it quite a joke, but Tara, the cook, reached the other side in a half-fainting condition. All the necessary baggage was brought across, but the mules, alas, had to remain behind. We sent them a five days' journey downstream where they were to cross the river and meet us on the other side.

Meanwhile I was obliged for the time being to have recourse to man-power as a carrying agency, a thing to which I have a rooted objection. But there was no choice. So as soon as the tents were pitched I sent the man whom the Rajah had lent me for such emergencies, to the nearest village with a message that I wanted half a dozen lusty fellows the next morning to carry the baggage. This meant dragging bales of 50-60 lbs. up hill by paths where a European might thank his stars if he could get himself to the top, let alone his impedimenta.

Before 5 a.m. I was awakened by the sound of talking, chattering and giggling, and Santoo trying in vain to put a stop to it. I opened the door of my tent to find my coolies sitting close in front of it in a semi-circle waiting to see what was going to happen. And then to my surprise I discovered one old man, two old women, two younger women, and a girl under fourteen. Evidently all the men we had notified had preferred to send their wives and daughters! They seem to have considered the work far too heavy for their good selves to tackle.

There is a general cry of "Salaam Sahib! Salaam Mem-Sahib!" most of the women folding their hands and bowing their heads. They stare in amazement at my wife. Then one woman creeps nearer and shakes out a number of nuts from the corner of her shawl. Our toilet excites the greatest astonishment. "Why! They are actually washing in cold water! Did you ever hear of such a thing!" And the brushing of teeth draws forth peals of laughter, though it is a thing that my servants are most particular about. They always carry with them a little stick with one end chewed into a tassel and make use of it after every meal.

When our tablecloths are spread in front of the tent the company withdraws a little and watches with the keenest interest the transference of every morsel from plate to mouth. Apparently they have never yet beheld fork, knife or spoon in use! We don't grudge the poor things such a treat, and meanwhile amuse ourselves by examining their ornaments and watching the ever-varying expression of their faces. For these people are of course totally unaccustomed to hide their feelings.

Another thing that elicits shrieks of surprise is the operation of striking our tent, especially when this palace is stowed away into a bag measuring 24 × 16 inches. When it is quite ready one of the young women rises, cords it round with a couple of ropes and, lying down alongside, binds the whole affair on to her back. She then gets up and walks off perkily amid the cheers of her companions. The old man then picks out the lightest load for himself, while the young girl takes possession of my knapsack. We try to make her understand that she must stick close to me as my camera is in it and I may want it at any moment. Not one of the six understands a single word of Hindustani, let alone English. But they are particularly sharp at signs, so that we are very soon on excellent terms. On the way we meet the 'mayor.' He understands Hindustani and amongst other things informs me that the carrier of my knapsack is a nun! That is why the poor creature is so shaven and shorn, her hair, women's chief glory in this country, being cropped short above the nape of the neck. All the others wear a long black plait liberally anointed with oil. Its length is increased by the plaiting-in of black strands of wool ending in a coloured woollen tassel which is often adorned with gold and silver thread.

The little girl is mortally afraid of me, and when I approached her to get my camera she trotted away in such a hurry that the mayor had to tell her she must come to me whenever I beckoned for it. She appears to be the wag of the party and keeps them all in good tune.

We advance in the best of spirits, the road being pretty good at first. Now and then there is an icy stream to cross, but our way mostly lies between sunny orchards where we soon meet with apricot trees. The fruit is instantly confiscated in large quantities by the mayor so that we can let the whole company feast upon it.

After two hours' tramp we reach the next village. Here all packs are deposited on the ground and all hands outstretched. We fail to understand the meaning of this until the mayor, who seems to take it all as a matter of course, tells us that this lot of carriers is not going further. They have done their duty and he must now look out for another set. A nice waste of time! I pay the coolies twopence a head inclusive of tips and treat the mayor to a piece of my mind, impressing upon him that he simply must secure some stalwart young men, and as soon as possible, unless he wishes the wrath of the British Raj to descend upon his unworthy head. Off he goes bowing and clasping his hands. Half an hour's interval. Then the coolies arrive without the mayor. Again they are women with only one man to look after them. My knapsack-bearer this time is a buxom dame with a dozen ear-rings in each ear, a gold clasp on her lip, and a gold nose-button. She has but one eye and a goitre as big as my fist. Her garments are tattered and patched to a surprising degree and unspeakably dirty. She is one of the *élite* of the village and has evidently put on these old clothes for rough work. This coolie transport-service is 'forced' labour which the villagers are called upon to perform by the mayor. You cannot refuse, though you may send your wife or daughter in your place. And this the gentlemen seem only too ready to do!

This set of workers also acquits itself admirably. In five hours they have scrambled up to tree-level between 3000-4000 feet along a boulder-strewn path over the stony slopes. They are barefoot of course. Occasionally we have the relief of a cedar wood, but for the most part the ascent is made in broiling sunshine.

At last we come to a suitable camping ground, though

'suitable' is a mild term. It is absolutely one of the most beautiful spots on which I have ever pitched my tent! A level grass plot on the outskirts of a great cedar forest where a gently rippling brook affords unlimited supplies of water, crystal clear. At the southern corner the ground rises four or five feet into a little terrace lying among lofty pines and commanding an unimpeded view, over meadows and cedar woods, of the giant peaks beyond. To the right, behind the camp, is a deep gulley out of which huge masses of white clouds are perpetually rising and travelling slowly up the mountainside to the crest of Kailas. There the forests cease. Save for a grassy slope here and there it is all bald and barren rock. The uprush of hot air from the burning rock-surfaces causes the clouds on reaching the summit to gyrate. Eddying, they slowly rend asunder and disperse, and dissolving into vapour are lost in the vault of heaven, against whose blue profundity the snows of Kailas stand out in white and sparkling radiance. High above the camp soars the Holy Mountain, its enormous snowfields, blue-green glaciers and russet rocks all contributing to a picture that has imprinted itself upon my memory as one of the loveliest of our whole tour. And one not recorded by memory alone, but fortunately in a measure by the camera, as the frontispiece to this volume shows.

Here we take leave of our coolies. Three days later a fresh contingent of these remarkable workers on the *corvée* system are to help us down again.

A wooded slope rises steeply just behind the camp, and we hear the wind from afar raging and howling across it. But with us there is not a breath stirring, and the smoke of our big fires rises steadily into the air. A short reconnaissance soon convinces us that we shall be able to reach an altitude of about 18,000 feet on the shoulder according to the plan we had worked out from the other side of the valley.

The next morning is of course splendidly fine. It is always fine here. And at early dawn we are stepping out through the cool mountain air in which one can manage to keep going at a smart pace, a great advantage as we have another 3000-4000 feet to climb. Above the wood we come to the region of alpine roses. Blue-throats innumerable are singing everywhere, and redstarts and pipits. Now and then a partridge calls. Snow pigeons are flying overhead. We are again among typical mountain scenery. A lovely *erica*, a species of heather, is a striking feature here, quite unknown on the other side of the valley. Its pure white blossoms with contrasting stamens of a beautiful orange-yellow bear us company all the way up, together with dwarf asters, and of course all kinds of saxifrages. The mountain-ridge, which we reach in a couple of hours, appears to be composed almost entirely of a fine white granular granite. Following it in a northerly direction we come to the first snows. To our left yawns a dizzy abyss. On our right a precipice as steep as a house. Sundry footprints and droppings indicate that the mountain sheep have made a track across the ridge. But these creatures are so timorous that it is well-nigh impossible to get a sight of them by daylight.

The ridge consists as usual of a series of peaks. We come to a halt on one of these, 18,000 feet high, the elevation of Mont Blanc, and looking round discover that our

KAILAS FROM THE FOREST ABOVE RIBBA

TEMPLE DANCE AT SARAHN

retinue is about a mile behind us. True, they are coming up, but with the utmost caution and deliberation. They are obviously frightened, and as soon as they get up to us positively refuse to go a step further. They have done their best they declare, have washed and bathed in the holy water that flows from the veil of Parbati, have prayed in so far as they knew how—but—they fear the resentment of their god should they venture unbidden to approach him nearer! And they rake up some dreadful stories about former travellers who have attempted to scale the heights of Kailas and of how only one ever returned to tell the tale!

And all the while there stands the great mountain behind us, bleak and forbidding in all its awful grandeur! How can one dream of making the ascent of slopes so precipitous, of crossing those vast expanses and walls of ice? We can see only Kailas from our halting place in the lee of the ridge, the more distant view being entirely hidden by the mountain range itself. But just a little beyond is another peak, which must be that given on the map with an altitude of 19,100 feet. It had attracted us from afar. At closer quarters it proves irresistible. It is a real mountain peak of steep pyramidal form and of difficult access from all sides. But there is a goat track leading right over the ridge.

So after a short rest for refreshment we start again. I am encumbered with my photographic apparatus and glasses, and have my coat on into the bargain, for the wind is howling over the ridge and the path is mostly on the side exposed to the blast. The track before us goes down a gentle incline and then rises by slow degrees to disappear inally at the foot of the pyramid. It is difficult to know what to do. The right-hand slope is full of great blocks of rock and intervening hollows filled with snow of a depth beyond computation. It is besides harassed by a bitterly piercing wind. On the left hand are steep rocks alternating with turfy ledges. We decide to take this difficult, but more sheltered, way rather than climb in the teeth of the wind over the rugged slopes.

We toil upwards painfully step by step, drawing breath with difficulty all the time, and picking our way with extreme caution, for beneath us yawns a chasm of many hundred feet. An alpenstock is of great service as an anchor on this steep incline. Here, with the snow-water trickling down from every crevice and the bleak wind screaming overhead, we come across a splendid mauve primula in full bloom with great succulent leaves. The only possible explanation of such a phenomenon on this arid steep is irrigation by the cold snow-water.

Photographing is no easy matter on such sharp gradients. First I have to find a good specimen of the plant required, and it must be on a place where I can stand safely and have my wife at hand to hold my knapsack or keep it steady. Then, everything being firmly fixed, I take out my camera and start the most hazardous part of the performance, *viz.* the focusing. And here let me advise every amateur photographer to take care what he is about. For remember that our equilibrium is maintained in a very large measure by visual impressions. Therefore, if you are standing on a narrow ledge and looking with both eyes into the reflex-camera, however little you may be inclined to dizziness you will be sure to wobble, for the sole and simple reason that you are looking at the landscape reversed, and thus any deviation from the normal in equilibrium is corrected reverse-wise in the brain. So you have to support yourself by knee or elbow, and then you may just manage to focus.

However, I was successful on this occasion and, somewhat out of breath, we repacked the camera. The last part of the way was very heavy going, and when we finally had to turn towards the wind damp masses of cloud blew straight into our faces. We could see them coming from afar. First they approach one by one and envelop us only for a few seconds. These are the vanguard of a gathering host of rapidly swelling cumuli that soon overshrouds the entire landscape. We have a momentary vision of Raldang, then of Kailas and of Jistingrung. Then only the two latter are visible by turns. At the summit we find a cairn of stones and prayer-flags, showing that shepherds and pilgrims have been there before us. Still the clouds prevail. Now and then part of a peak or a glacier, a snowfield or a precipice, will emerge. But there is nothing like a panorama of the range. We are lucky, however, to have at least three-quarters of the horizon unencumbered by hurrying clouds. At a depth of 15,000 feet below lies the sunlit valley of the Sutlej. On the other side of it are Chini and our late camping-ground on Chini Kanda, the fields from which we made our first ascents and the peaks with which we are already familiar. North of Kailas there is a clear view, for all the clouds that draw over and about us caught by the hot air rising from the sun-scorched rock surfaces eddy and slowly vanish into the sky. Away there, beyond our camp,

Thibet is visible in the blue haze of distance, the mighty crest of Pir Panjal forming a great natural boundary-post upon its frontier. This is one of the finest peaks of the region with its prodigious gradient of 18,000 feet in every six and a quarter miles. Beside it lies the famous Spiti valley on Anglo-Indian soil, whose inhabitants are Thibetans of pure Mongolian type. For a whole hour we sit here gazing out over the universe—this wonderful world which holds so much in store. And we form our plans and dream our dreams of some day journeying yonder into Kashmir. But when? Ah, when!

But at this height the clammy moisture from the clouds is an increasing source of discomfort and forbids further lingering. So we take our way downhill again, this time along the windward slope, alternately bathed in sunshine or wading deep in thick mist. We discovered our servants in the act of prayer. I fancy they had almost given us up and were immensely relieved when we appeared. We got back to camp in good spirits as usual. But to this day I remember the toughness of that old fowl for which the mayor had charged us between three and four shillings.

The next day the coolies arrived punctually. This time there were six women under the command of the youngest, a pretty child of sixteen or so, who if you please was carrying about 12 lbs. weight of gold in her necklace, and another two and thirty attached to a string in company with her door-key. She also wore massive gold bracelets and ditto ear-rings to the number of a dozen or more. This heiress actually consented to carry the bale containing our tent some 1800 feet up hill, and another 5600 feet or so down, walking from 6 a.m. till 4 p.m. over rough ground and gritty trackless slopes, and later right through the jungle, and all for the sum of less than three shillings and sixpence! What was more, the coolies were all delighted with the pay. I gave each of them an extra shilling for doing their job so well, and I may say for chattering and laughing all the time. Whereupon the whole lot of them fell on their knees, folded their hands and touched the ground and our feet with their foreheads. When after this we sent them off with a pound of apricots apiece, we distinctly saw that they thought we were not quite right in the top storey.

At last by break-neck paths we come down again from the region of bare rock to the apricot orchards where the corn is standing nearly two feet high. At Shontong the mules, having made the round, are waiting for us, and we proceed further downstream, but not by a pleasant riverside path by any means. At every instant we are confronted with rocks which necessitate our climbing some hundreds of feet above the path and then diving down again. On these precipitous places the road is abominably bad. Such level portions as there are have been obtained for the most part by blasting the rock, for the course of the river is often in a gulley with almost perpendicular rocks on either hand. We go *viâ* Kilba to Sholtu, there rejoining our former road. But now we generally camp in the gardens of the Forest bungalows or put up at the rest houses. Splendid institutions these. Directly we arrive, a table and chairs are brought to the camping-ground. Then a big bouquet of flowers regularly makes its appearance, with a basket of apricots and apples and another large one of vegetables for the kitchen. At the same time coolies arrive with straw and firewood. And then comes the *chowkidar* or keeper, with a *chit* from the Deputy-Sub-Assistant-Forestry-Commissioner or someone of that kind to ask if he can be of any service to us. This is what I call being really helpful. There is no doubt the English know how to do things properly.

CHAPTER IX

THE RETURN JOURNEY

We are now tramping back along the same old road. The same, and yet not the same, for the rainy season has begun, and directly we cross the Wangtu Bridge there are traces everywhere of a heavy deluge. The clouds are still low and we are constantly walking through mist. But the rain has really worked miracles. Not that there are many flowers, for pollen is affected by water. But all the sides of the valley are flushed with fresh green. Myriads of insects are astir, particularly beetles, and, most noteworthy fact of all, the natives themselves are preparing for a change! This is the month when the native gods, whose sacrificial feast I have already described, are setting forth on their travels. In all the temple courts as we pass there is music and dancing going on, and we constantly meet caravans of pilgrims when we go to visit sick people in the hills. For people are perpetually coming to the camp from distances of three or four miles to get medical advice for their sick folk. On one occasion the 'Cheldar' of Bari, a sort of provincial chieftain, came imploring us to go to his wife and sister who were both ill. These people are absolutely cut off from all medical aid and totally ignorant in matters of hygiene. As we were on our way to Bari we were called in to visit an old man who, according to his son, had fallen down and broken his arm, and his leg, and his lower jaw! Of course I couldn't discover the least trace of a fracture about him. In such cases a little ointment on the bruises and a tabloid of aspirin work wonders. Meanwhile faith in the remedies is always a help towards recovery.

This special visit gave us an opportunity we should not otherwise have had of visiting a village off the beaten track. The roads in most cases here only skirt the villages. All the houses in this place were of two storeys, the upper storey having a large balcony, or rather verandah. From a distance they looked quite pretty, many of the verandahs being decorated with carving. But on closer inspection you discover that the lower storey is only a stable in which sheep and goats, milch goats as well as others, and a couple of yoke oxen all live happily together. The manure from the stable is dumped in a heap in front of the open door mingling with that which is thrown down from above. This is all there is in the way of drain or privy. The result is an indescribable state of beastliness. By means of the verandah you gain access to the living-rooms through an entrance so low that you are forced to bend nearly double, and once inside have to sit on your heels. The rooms, which measure only about 7 × 11 feet, are empty except for a few old rags in one corner that do duty for a bed, while in another corner is a clutter of copper pots and pans, the family kitchen and table utensils. Some of the dishes are beautifully wrought and the goblets are of copper with a silver foot. The rest of the family property will be found as usual hanging round the necks or in the ears and noses of the women.

While I visited the sick man my wife was treated to apricots and nuts, and a little fire of burning cow-dung was placed between her feet, for at that early hour of the morning it was still chilly. Besides, the fire kept off the flies. On leaving, we were presented with large quantities of nuts and sweet apricot kernels.

Then we went on to Bari, which entailed another climb of an hour and a half by an awful path. One ragamuffin carried the medicine chest, a dusky young damsel shouldered my knapsack, while my wife's butterfly net was triumphantly borne by a nun. On arrival, to our surprise, we were conducted to the sacred precincts of the temple, where we were again regaled with several pounds of apricots and more nuts. Meanwhile the entire population of the village had assembled outside. It might have been that never before had a Sahib nor, much less, a Mem-Sahib, set foot within the confines of Bari.

A stretcher was then brought in, garments were spread upon it, and we were invited to take our seats. However, we had already learned by bitter experience that it is better to sit upon stone than upon the finest garments of Kashmir! . . . Ugh! I can still feel them tickling! . . . So when the first patient—a woman—was carried in, she was deposited on the stretcher. It was fortunately possible to give a little relief to some dozen cases by binding up wounds, clearing out ulcers, bathing sore eyes, etc. Aspirin and quinine were also distributed. And then after giving some advice on the care of infants, and cutting the dirty nails of several children, the Sahib received from the Cheldar an honorarium in the shape of a copper dish and the Mem-Sahib was presented with a big silver shawl pin. A pretty attention. (*N.B.*—I may mention that there is no law here to forbid the pursuit of the healing art by unqualified practitioners !)

Back again we go down the hill, escorted by half the village; through mist and mizzle, uphill and downhill for a matter of five hours; till we arrive to find another *chowkidar* waiting for us with another offering of vegetables !

The next day is still cloudy with mist and drizzling rain, and we have to break our march half-way and light a roaring fire to dry ourselves. In another quarter of an hour we are as dripping wet as ever. That night at Sarahn we are treated to a downpour of seven hours on end. I had just time, before it began, to dig a gutter round our tent, but my partner's tent collapsed, as the pegs had no grip in the soppy ground. He slept through it all, however, till the water was up to his knees. In the morning more mist and fog. It is the monsoon, so the prospect for the next few months is not altogether pleasant. But our tea is warm at any rate, and 'The Homestead' (as I call our tent) has stood firm. So that is something.

Sarahn, or Sarahan, is the summer residence of the Rajah of Bashahr, the State of which I gave some details in the account of our arrival at Rampur. The Rajah, Padam Singh, has just made his entry into the village, so the place is crowded. As soon as our tent has been properly fixed up the Rajah's secretary arrives bidding us to the palace the following day at two o'clock. Just twenty-four hours in which to make ourselves presentable ! Quite a *tour de force* after six weeks in the wilderness, especially in a steady downpour of rain.

The palace in Sarahn, in shape, reminds one of a big wooden cuckoo-clock. It is all made up of laths and posts with ornamental props and struts everywhere. It is painted in gay colours and crammed with flowers and numbers of solemn white-turbaned officials. The Rajah himself is a simple, kindly man who, I must tell you, speaks not a word of English, so conversation with him is a somewhat tedious business. He professes the keenest interest in the results of our explorations, wanting particularly to know if we have found any minerals or precious stones. When I fail to reassure him on this point he then, after much beating about the bush, begins to consult me about his daughter-in-law. She is seriously ill—some affection of the bowels, with complications. Can I do anything for it ? I put a few questions and find that his own physician, an Indian doctor fresh from college, is away staying with a relative a fortnight's journey in the hills. "Besides," he adds, "I have very little confidence in him." A doctor from Simla has been consulted, but without avail. But if only the Mem-Sahib herself would just go and have a look at the invalid ? And I might go with her, but if I went into the room I must stand behind a screen! The Simla doctor had of course not been allowed to see the patient. And my further inquiries as to the colour of the lips and skin soon make it quite plain that His Highness himself has never set eyes on his daughter-in-law without her veil. So strict is the purdah-system among high-caste Hindus.

Later on it also becomes evident that the local Mrs. Grundys will think it improper to admit even the Mem-Sahib to the sick-room. Meanwhile the Rajah is so anxious to get medicine for the sick woman that I promise to send some back by his secretary who is to escort us home.

While talking these matters over we hear the " Ching-ching-*Boom* ! " of a jazz band, and lo ! to the accompaniment of sacred music, there approach three gods, with an escort of eight drums, four cymbalists, two gongs and six trumpets, two of them of the curved S-shaped variety. Properly speaking they are not trumpets at all, having neither mouthpiece nor keys ; they are really megaphones or loud-speakers. They blare forth a series of " ti-oo-oos," the last syllable an octave lower than the first.

The gods are of the same kind as before. Great shakos with masks below, though the latter in this case are not only of silver but also of tin and copper. Neither are they set with gems, as I presently perceive when the Rajah beckons me to a nearer view from the terrace. Evidently these are poor gods from the neighbourhood who are coming to pay a visit to him. His Highness slightly inclines his head and folds his hands as the three images are aligned before us, a deafening din of " ching ching-*Boom*-ti-oo-oo " going on all the time. Then they are borne off see-sawing and dancing on their bamboo poles all round the square. When we see them turn in the direction of the temple we take our leave of the Rajah and, promising to come if possible to the Rampur Fair in October, we make our way to the temple court.

Here a crowd has assembled bright with colour. All the women wear headcloths and sleeveless jackets or bodices of brilliant hues, a great contrast to the jute garments of the hill folk. They are bedizened with gold and silver ear-rings and nose-rings and wear rings also on their toes. Faces of the Ladakh-Thibetan type are less common here, the prevailing cast of countenance being of the Semitic-Arabian order.

We have just time to install ourselves on a sort of balcony, upon two chairs from the telephone office, when the musicians, who have paused to refresh themselves with sacred wine from the temple, start again. The steady downpour of rain seems in no way to damp the festive spirit of the crowd, and the men and women rapidly form themselves into a long chain, one hand in front and one behind, just as we do for skating. Preceded by the band they then dance round the gods in a kind of three-step—three forward and two back—with a curtseying movement of the knees. The drummers on arriving in front of our rostrum toss up their drums and, giving just a touch to steady them, carry them balanced on their heads. The dancers now go through some paces under the leadership of the high priest; the drummers and horn blowers take a couple of turns gesticulating fiercely; and then the whole motley crew moves on again in time to a regular measure.

At this moment comes a gleam of sunshine. Everything sparkles with colour and we catch a glimpse of the glaciers between the stupendous masses of cloud. Before we reach home the clouds have dwindled into mere fleecy puffs, through which the mountain tops and glaciers and snowfields are all distinctly visible. We all go out to take an airing after the rain and feel hopeful that for another day or two, or perhaps longer, we shall have fine weather. Santoo, however, is sceptical. And Santoo is right. An hour later the rain is again rattling down on the roof of our tents and the servants are splashing about the camping-ground ankle-deep in water.

At six o'clock the next morning, as we are at breakfast, there is another roll of drums followed by a "ti-oo-oo" louder and more distressfully wailing than any we have yet heard. Santoo runs off to find out what is the matter and returns with bad news. He begins by asking whether I sent any medicine yesterday to the Rajah and looks immensely relieved when I say "No." And then he announces that the royal invalid died last night and that her body is at this very moment being carried down to the banks of the sacred river to be burnt. Without waiting to hear another word we start off at once to pay our last respects to the dead, and meet the funeral procession just behind the camp. First come the silver trumpets, and then all the drums both from the temple and the village. These are followed by the bier, covered with red silk and adorned with paper flowers. It is borne by four Brahmins, four other priests holding over it, by way of canopy, a green silk shawl stretched on rough wooden sticks. For the sun is beating down fiercely and the day promises to be hot. The whole population of the village stands lining the way, the fact that a court official walks close behind the bier, throwing handfuls of annas to the bystanders, probably being one of the chief attractions. Most of the men fall in with the procession and follow it down a mule-path leading to the valley. Progress is by fits and starts, for the rain of the previous night has turned a great portion of the path into a stream of mud which causes a good deal of slipping and falling. At first we descend by a gentle incline, but the pitch gradually becomes steeper, till finally, after an hour and a half of tortuous and difficult going, we get down to the bed of the Sutlej. The river at

THE DEATH OF THE MAHRANEE PROCLAIMED BY A BLARE OF TRUMPETS

THE BIER WITH THE MUSICIANS

(*Face p.* 122.)

THE PROCESSION WINDING UP THE HILI

DESPOILING THE CORPSE

this point flows between high rocks, and a little further on foams into rushing rapids.

The bier is set down, and the Brahmins get to work to level a place for the funeral pyre in the gravel of the river-bed close to the water's edge. Others go into the forest to cut wood. In an hour or two they have made ready a pyre standing a good three feet from the ground with a surface measurement of about $3\frac{1}{2} \times 6\frac{1}{2}$ feet. Upon this they lay the body, still in its red silk covering. Then four Brahmins strip themselves naked and bathe in the ice-cold water, after which, standing by the side of the river to prevent any view of the corpse, they proceed to remove the silken covering and divest the dead woman of all her ornaments. Every Hindu woman here carries her ornaments with her at her death to the place of cremation. The Brahmins remove them and use them for their own benefit, by sale or otherwise. In the case of a man, his clothes, gold shirt-buttons, watch, etc., also become the spoil of the priest, who is always poor, and dependent on the charity of the faithful.

Still they keep bringing wood, and yet more wood, until there is a pile of over three feet above the red shawl. Then the oldest of the Brahmins draws forth a roll of parchment and begins to read aloud from the Vedas amid loud cries from the others for more and more wood, and resounding blows from the hatchets as the bier is hewn in pieces and cast on the funeral pyre or into the river. The reading of the prayers continues while oil is poured over the pyre and sacred cedar-wood from Benares added to the fuel. And then at last, all the funeral flowers having been removed, the Brahmins take bunches of dried grass and set fire to the pyre from all four sides at once.

All this time the band has kept up a deafening row increasing in intensity while the last rites are performed. Now, as the first flames shoot upwards, the music is suddenly hushed. The ceremony is at an end.

No members of the family followed the bier. Everything was in the hands of the priests and nothing was prepared beforehand. No wood ready, no hatchets. Three Brahmins selected places for the pyre and then squabbled over which was the best. They all laughed and sang as they cut and carried the wood. No one paid the slightest attention to the sacred words read by the high priest, and once he was nearly knocked down by a coolie with a faggot. All present appeared to be wearing their worst rags, such 'old clo' as none of our beggars would dare show his face in. One of the musicians had actually left his instrument behind at a wayside spring, and when the lighting of the funeral pyre was heralded by a special flourish of "ti-oo-oos" addressed through rams' horns to all four quarters of the compass, our friend blared abroad a separate tootle of his own through his closed fists.

And so the flames blaze high above the lonely corpse of one for whom existence has never meant aught but dread seclusion; who living has known little of the joys of life. And as they blaze, lesser fires are kindled round about, and *japati* is cooked, and there is card-playing, and jokes and jollity.

Presently, when the fire has died down, the oldest of the Brahmins will consign the ashes to the river, first re-

THE CONCLUSION OF THE CEREMONY

THE CAPPARIS, A ROCK SHRUB

(*Face p.* 124.)

THE DOOR OF THE TEMPLE, SARAHN

moving a small piece of the skull. This bit of bone will be placed in a silver-mounted casket and taken by the priests to Hardwar on the Ganges and there deposited in the family tomb of the Rajahs of Bashahr.

. . . .

Rain, rain, rain! And rain it is with a vengeance. A regular market-day thunderstorm. The sort of thing that goes on for three or four hours, or may last as much as twenty-four. And this in a land of hills and valleys and precipitous paths! No wonder that roads are washed away, their banks collapsing into landslides, or that one's way is frequently blocked by brooks in spate, dealing havoc in their course. But for all that the rain is a blessing. The arid mountain-slopes of our outward journey, so parched and sun-stricken that the labour of building them into terraces seemed strangely ill-bestowed, are now being ploughed by oxen wading through shallow water. There are men busy planting rice, stooping for hours in the rain and pressing the young plants into the ooze in irregular lines. Paddy fields are showing green, and every gleam of sunshine is reflected in innumerable twinkling water-meadows.

Our present road leads downhill and downstream, the air growing more sultry the further we descend. In the rare intervals of sunshine the atmosphere is that of a hot-house. Occasional bananas lend a tropical character to the villages nestling among fig-trees in the midst of the rice fields, and there is a wealth of young green on the barren stems of the giant euphorbias, which here are plants of cactus-like appearance and shrubby growth. Wandering all over the rice fields are apes, many of them with their young in ridiculous attitudes on their backs. The apes pillage the fig-trees and bananas, and ere long will start their depredations on the rice fields, unhindered by the natives who, as I have said, regard these plagues as sacred. And so we go on until we arrive at Luri, which lies just below our old halting-place Narkanda.

The road now winds uphill for hours at an incline of about 3700 feet in six to seven miles. The sky is overcast, and by the time we approach Kunmarsain it has become oppressively hot. So hot that the partridges are silent in the ripe corn and the apes, from sheer torpor, allow us to get within six feet or so, when they dart, hoarsely screeching, into the trees.

Kunmarsain, capital of a Native State of the same name, is a small straggling village. Two of the streets are paved with large flag-stones, a unique phenomenon north of Simla. The Rajah's palace on the brow of the hill is a remarkable jumble of about six different styles of architecture, but it is brand new and looks fairly clean. We soon find a camping site in the pine-woods above the village, and the Rajah, in sending us permission to pitch our tents there, adds that he will be pleased to receive us whenever we like to call, and the earlier the better. The bearer of his gilt-edged missive reports that we have no tables and chairs in the camp, and so a quarter of an hour later seven coolies appear toiling up the hill, three of them with a chair apiece, and the other four groaning under the weight of quite the biggest and heaviest table I have ever beheld. A sort of double-decker affair, glazed cupboard and tea-table combined, measuring 5 × 9 feet with leaves an inch and a half thick. A really sumptuous piece of furniture.

We wait on His Highness at 2.30 and spend two hours and a half in conversation with him. He is a well educated man of animated appearance, speaking excellent English and interested in all that goes on in the world. His secretary, who also took part in the conversation, had been up in Thibet with Sven Hedin and had much to say about that country and its inhabitants. And what was more, he really displayed a thorough knowledge of both.

The Rajah began with a few civil inquiries about our journey, and asked whether we had everything we required. He took the lead in conversation, and we soon noticed that he never missed a chance of picking the brains of everyone he came across. Directly he found out that I had studied chemistry he started a whole string of questions. Could I advise him how to help on agriculture a little? And what did I think of his country? When I told him, he next overwhelmed me with questions about manures and selection of suitable seed, how to grapple with weeds, the prevention and cure of diseases in plants, and so on. Questions to which I was naturally unable to give more than superficial answers. So I recommended him if possible to get a few students from the Forest College in Lahore and appoint them as officials in his State. He told us that he had already tried this on his own initiative, but that his subjects were so strongly averse from any innovations that he had bethought himself of a still better plan. It seems that the ten best scholars from the Government school—the secondary school—at Kunmarsain are always sent at his expense to study for two years at Lahore. What he now intended was that they should go through a course at the Agricultural College. He would then appoint them as instructors in the village schools to teach the labourers' children something more practical than English history and geography. In the same way he had sent some of the girls, also at his own cost, to the technical schools and hospitals, that the knowledge so acquired might be employed for the benefit of the state.

Well done, Rajah Sahib! One only regrets that his territory is of such small extent. However, the British Government is aware of what he is doing and will doubtless hold him up as an example to the rulers of far larger states.

We then got on to politics. It was not surprising to find the Rajah complain of the way in which the Government insists on forcing an Englishman as chief official upon every native state. At the same time he freely admitted that British supremacy was indispensable, and that if the whites were to leave India the whole country would fall a prey to internal dissensions.

And so we went on talking, passing from politics to questions of educational reform and finally to sport. When we left, the Rajah offered us three saddle-horses for the stiff climb on the following day, a proposal we accepted with some hesitation, as we are but poor riders!

The next morning the weather looked threatening. Our Rosinantes arrived, and fortunately appeared to be fairly meek. The only drawback, so far as I was concerned, was that the stirrups were too small for my shoes. Nevertheless, when the rain began to fall in torrents and continued for three hours, during the whole of the 3700 feet ascent to Narkanda, I was devoutly thankful to sit comfortably in my mackintosh and just let myself be dragged up the hill.

We returned by the familiar road through the dusky Narkanda pine-woods, the rain still steadily pouring and mist enveloping us for hours together. After that, out of pure exasperation with the weather, we just tore over the last forty miles from Narkanda to Simla. The consequence of that ride was that I was unable to sit for a couple of days. . . .

At Simla, more rain and mist. It is much worse than our autumn at home because the weather changes so quickly. At ten o'clock you may get glorious sunshine and have all the windows and doors wide open. In another five minutes the mist will come billowing down, followed a little later by torrents of rain. Everything becomes damp and mildewy. Your postage-stamps and your photographs stick together, and all your envelopes get sealed up. Clothes and bedding are clammy and smell fusty. If you put on warm clothes, a burning sun makes you stream with perspiration. If you are lightly clad, your teeth chatter with the chill of the fog, or a cold rain drenches you to the skin. It is really past human endurance. So off we start for the plains. The train rushes us swiftly back to Delhi and Agra and Bombay, and south again to Hyderabad and Cuddapoor and Madras. And then, still under torrential rain or through heat like that in a hot-house, to Madura, an oasis in a wilderness of fig-trees and cactus plants. We have now left the monsoon behind us. We feel dry again and set open our trunks to air. Then on through Tinnevelly and Quilon, until after six nights in the train, having had one day's interval in Bombay, another in Madras, and a few hours in Madura to stretch our legs, we reach the terminus of the Indian

State Railway at Trivandrum, the capital of Travancore, at 8° from the equator, Simla, our starting point, being at a northern latitude of 32°. And here I must leave the story of our travels ' to be continued in our next.'

PART II

THE AUTUMN TOUR

CHAPTER I

THE HIMALAYAS AGAIN

We are again speeding northwards by express train across the vast plains of India. The desert of our first journey is now transformed into a paradise of luxuriant vegetation springing up everywhere after the monsoon. The immeasurable wastes are covered with millet and maize and sugar canes, all standing, like the grass, six or seven feet high. It is still pretty hot although the middle of October, and we draw a breath of relief as the motor brings us swiftly up from Kalka in the Plains to the cedar woods of Simla. Here the vegetation is quite dried up. The beautiful forests of ferns, which the rain prevented us photographing in the middle of August, now lie like masses of hay, drooping under the trees. In the daytime the sun is hot, but the nights are quite chilly, so that we shall have to take blankets with us presently when we return to the mountains.

Before starting we spend a couple of days in Simla to acclimatize ourselves and make preparations for the journey, also to assist at a big religious festival. At a run of an hour and a half from Simla, on a high hill known as Tara Devi, there is a temple of Kali, the Goddess of Death, built to commemorate an event whose anniversary is celebrated every year.

It will be remembered that I previously related a legend in connection with the apes, of how Rama, the prophet, went to conquer Ceylon in order to recover his wife from her captors. Now it so happened that he encountered in battle a giant, to whom the gods had granted this favour: that from each drop of his blood that should fall to the ground a son would arise to aid him in the strife. Rama fought like a lion, but as fast as he decapitated one son, two others appeared in his place. The gods on Kailas, seeing that their divine emissary was getting the worst of it, besought Kali to help him. Kali thereupon entered into the fray and caught in her mouth each giant's blood-drops as they flowed from the blows of Rama's sword. And thus Rama won the day. This feat of arms is still annually commemorated in most towns and villages of British India on the 16th of October, when many thousands flock to the nearest Kali temple. They generally combine the function with a kind of fair, at which a variety of merchandise is exposed for sale along the side of the road, sweetmeats and bracelets appearing to be the chief commodities. No Rajah will omit to visit the temple of Kali on this day.

Unfortunately we did not happen to strike a good moment for our visit, the Rajah of Koti having that year for the first time forbidden the sacrifice. As it is almost unthinkable that this feast of all others should be held without bloodshed, it was not surprising that on this occasion there were barely a thousand spectators present instead of some ten thousand. They were busy enjoying themselves at the swings and the sweet stalls, or engaged in the favourite sport of beating the drum. A remarkable pastime this. A big temple drum, similar to our kettle-drums, is belaboured with cudgels in time to a rhythm set by a couple of smaller drums. For a few pence you may bang away till you drop. Most Hindus get so excited over this game that they can only keep it up about ten minutes. A love of showing-off naturally plays a large part in the business.

We wandered round among the happy band of pilgrims for an hour or so. The women were tremendously tricked out with gold and silver ornaments as may be seen by the accompanying photograph. But the real festival spirit was lacking as there was no culminating point in the ceremony, and the Brahmins muttered among themselves that Kali would most likely take her revenge. They muttered still more when the Rajah presently arrived not in full dress, and without that outward pomp and circumstance to which Orientals are so addicted. Whether Kali actually did take her revenge I never heard.

Two days later we again bid farewell to civilisation. The heavy rains at the end of July had so interfered with our geological observations that our first object now was to visit the Sutlej Valley close to Simla, and the country in the vicinity, and then to work our way northwards as far as Rampur, making an especial inclusion of the tributary rivers in our programme.

We begin with a day's march of fifteen miles straight up the valley to Seoni and pitch our first camp at an altitude of about 3700 feet on the valley's edge. We had left at an early hour and the first part of the way led by a rapid descent through a superb forest where we started several pheasants and kept coming across birds which we had not previously met with. These were evidently migrants, and the first lot sent to our ornithologist friend

THE BELLE OF THE VILLAGE

(*Face p.* 134.)

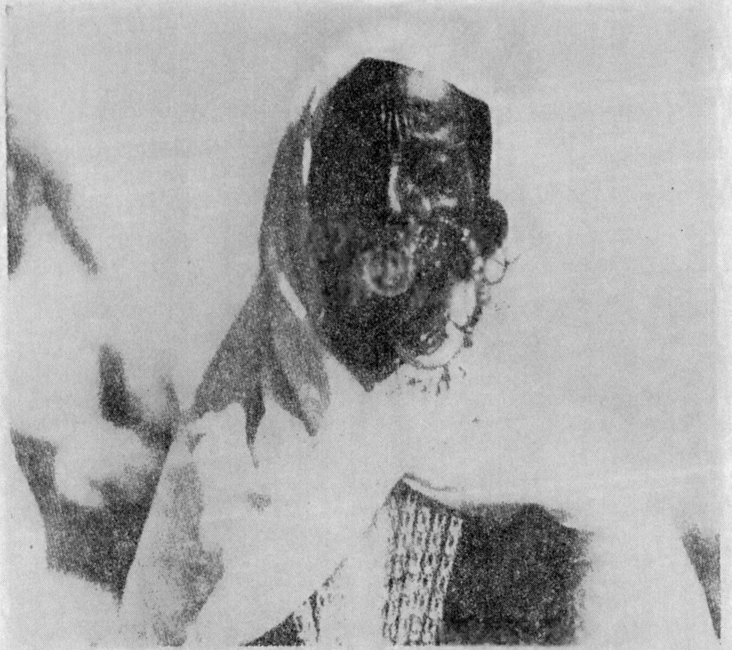

OMA

GOAT WITH YOUNG ON ITS BACK

in Simla comprised some birds of a typical Thibetan species.

Our servants are the same old set, with the exception of the cook, who had left, as Santoo and Jittoo said they could quite well manage the cooking and it would give more room in the tent, besides being much cheaper for us. As we always spent so much time on the way collecting geological and ornithological specimens, the servants said they might easily start an hour later and catch us up. We were therefore able to walk at our leisure and give our feet a chance to get accustomed to the mountain shoes and the mountain paths. We began our day by finding some fine examples of limestone formation, totally unexpected here so close to Simla, and our unhurried observations took so much time that it was five o'clock when we got to the camping place. But not a sign of either servants or mules! Six o'clock came, and the sun went down. While we were sitting in the dark by a small fire feeling very hungry, a troop of Indians alighted at the spring hard by. They actually invited us to share their meal, and a moment later we were munching *japati* with *dall* and onions and peppered potatoes, all prepared for us by no less a personage than the Head Revenue Officer. He cooked the meal over a wood fire beneath an ilex tree, in one of the jolly copper pots that everyone uses here. These gentlemen had taken the opportunity of a few days' leave to make an excursion to the hot springs near Seoni, and they declared themselves much honoured by the Sahib and the Mem-Sahib (the woman here always takes the second place) having consented to share their repast.

At eight o'clock, by the light of a full moon, the first of

our servants appears upon the scene, the mules arriving an hour later. By nine-thirty all the tents are up and the camp sunk in profound repose, with the exception of the mules, who wander about all night in the moonlight chewing maize straw and making a noise like a steam corn-mill at work. At least, so it sounds in the stillness of the night.

The next morning we make an excursion to the power-station which supplies the lighting of Simla, eighteen miles away and 7500 feet higher than this spot. The electricity is chiefly generated by the water-power of a large stream, a tributary of the Sutlej.

The river is certainly about fifteen to twenty feet lower than it was in August, and this being the first time we have been so far down stream our attention is attracted by some very interesting stone-formations. All this part of the river bed and the sides of the valley consist of limestone exhibiting a variety of whimsically fantastic shapes, as its resistant properties being less than those of the far harder granite, it is consequently more readily subject to erosion.

We next proceed to the warm springs. These are an extraordinary phenomenon. The hot water comes bubbling up from the gravel of the river bed, which is under water during the monsoon. You only have to scoop out a hole in the gravel and your bath is ready. Of course there is an effervescence of sulphuretted hydrogen with the familiar smell of rotten eggs, but the Hindus don't appear to mind this. For that matter, any invalid who is ordered sulphur baths may be well content to put up with it. The spring gives forth a great volume of water. Here and there the stream collects in separate pools among the rocks and, depend upon it, if this spot were not so remote it would become an important watering-place. You can have baths both hot and cold and a "banana" cure if you like, besides abundance of game shooting. The place is romantically situated close to the river, which here rushes foaming through a wild and rocky ravine. And those who think it too far to cross by the bridge can avail themselves of a very interesting method of transit. Two inflated cow hides are tied together, and upon them is lashed a kind of couch for the convenience of invalids. The ordinary native, however, just flings himself across the cow and crosses the river by paddling with his hands and steering with his feet. If you happen to be in a hurry you can go across sitting astride a native's back, the chance being a hundred to one on your reaching the other side in safety. But that one chance means death in the foaming rapids of the ravine. Even under present conditions a visit to Seoni may be of great help to sufferers from rheumatism, that is if they can manage the two days' walk in the heat by such a difficult road. The rheumatism seems actually to disappear of itself, as it were.

Our camp here is on a piece of rising meadowland by the river. Behind us are some giant bamboos and a few banana trees, the young leaves of which Santoo promptly turns to account by cutting them in pieces to serve as dinner-plates, thus saving himself the trouble of washing up. He had of course cribbed the idea from what he had seen in the markets of Southern India. There are other things also that remind us of the sun-scorched plains. First of all the bamboos. And a little further on the road is overshadowed by a giant Waringin or banyan tree. And on the river slopes are numbers of date-palms. The fruit of these is, however, not at all palatable, the trees having grown up from seeds sown by the birds. The latter, when migrating to northern climes, let fall the stones which, I may incidentally mention, do not pass through the digestive tract, but are ejected through the beak of the bird some hours after the fruit has been caten. One notices our hooded crows doing the same thing with the wild hips. These date-palms are of luxuriant growth and a great adornment to the banks of the river, but they require proper cultivation and above all ample supplies of water. With these they could certainly be made to produce edible fruit.

Our camp is shaded by a narrow-leaved eucalyptus of the familiar Australian type, the same whose powcrful odour so often pervades our happy homes about Christmas time. While we are sitting at dinner a dark shadow suddenly alights on the end of a branch. My gun happens to be lying handy. Bang! goes the shot, and lo! fluttering in our soup tureen lies a bat, and what is more a bat of the kalong or flying-fox variety, a visitor from the south. Its wings when spread out measure more than three feet from tip to tip. Another fine specimen for our collection.

Our plan now is to go upstrcam along the bed of the Sutlej as far as possible and at the same time take a good look at the side-rivers. It appears fairly easy to combine the two, as both banks of the Sutlej are so precipitous that in places there is actually no room for a road. This happens for instance just above Seoni, where we have to go up one of the side-rivers, then over the watersheds of two or three others until we can reach a place where the map shows another mule track leading back to the main river and continuing upstream for several miles. After that, advance again becomes impossible and we have to climb up 8000 feet to dive down another 2400 feet on the further side of the ridge into the next valley.

The following morning while we were having tea more visitors arrived in the shape of two great black birds that came winging their way in a straight line and plunged down into the stream in front of us. Cormorants! those remarkable birds that still breed on many of our cliffs at home, though gradually becoming extinct in the more western parts of Europe. In China these birds have for ages been employed by the inhabitants for fishing, but the present specimens are at work on their own account. Drifting swiftly with the current, they keep diving under the water just as they do in Europe, and frequently a twisting movement down the front of the long neck betokens that another lusty fish has just been gulped.

At the same moment I spot through the glasses another old friend, the sand martin. Dozens of these pretty little creatures, with brownish plumage and white underside, are wheeling through the air above a sunny slope of sand across the river. There is a good deal of sand here. On the first terrace by the riverside there are even little dunes of it at intervals, with their usual concomitant of coarse bents. Wheatears are here and turtle doves and all kinds of other birds of suggestively homelike appearance. And last, but not least, our old friend the 'magpie robin,' a red-breasted variety of magpie. When we were in Travancore this little bird used to enliven our breakfast-table every morning with his song.

A few hours later we start off in good heart for our first hill-climbing expedition, using an unfrequented and dreadfully steep path. However, the going is fairly good, in spite of the sweltering heat of the sun on our backs. It is a worse business getting down on the other side. We have to tread gingerly, hopping from stone to stone, and as most of the stones here are inclined to roll we are constantly pulled up short when preparing to spring. It is warm work and very fatiguing, and the annoying part of it is that having to be perpetually hunting for the safest spot to plant your feet you have absolutely no chance whatever of looking about you. If you want to see a bird or get a glimpse of a peak it is a matter of clapping on the brake with a vengeance. So altogether that first day we don't get far, and end by camping at an early hour a few miles up the small river that supplies the power-station. Here we amuse ourselves by catching fish in an original manner taught us by a half-naked dryad in Travancore. The recipe is a simple one. You take a shallow copper bowl and bind it up in a duster in which you make a round hole of about one inch in diameter. Into the bowl you put some cooked rice and raw meat, and smear a little cheese or cooked brains round the hole. The fish first lick the cloth clean and then go inside, and in about half an hour if you raise the trap from the water you generally find a dozen or more fishes guzzling in the bowl. In this way we were enabled to 'pot' some nice trout and other fish, that is to say preserve them in spirits for the Amsterdam Museum. Santoo took the remainder, chopped them up fine with skin and bones, and served them as croquettes. Large fish don't seem to go into the trap. Though we left the bowl out all night, the following morning we had caught nothing but two crabs. Crabs are a queer sight up here in the hills. But we had seen far too many of them caught by a great vulture in the rice fields of Travancore to take kindly to the idea of crabs in fresh water. But any way it was an unexpected haul, and after all we weren't obliged to have them in croquettes as fortunately there was still half a chicken left, the last we should see for a week.

Next day we climbed the hill to the watershed to get over into the bed of the next stream. We had made a point of being under way betimes, so as not to be inconvenienced by the sun in making the ascent. Nevertheless it was pretty warm, and thankful indeed we were to cool ourselves with pomegranates and the berries of a kind of *berberis* which grows plentifully along the road. In all directions you hear hidden partridges calling in the high standing corn. Sometimes we come across goats and sheep laden with sacks of salt. Some of them have their young ones with them, one little mother carrying her precious burden on her back. Her young kids are not yet big enough to spring over the steep slopes and keep up with the rest of the flock. So the herdsman has packed the little things up in a couple of salt sacks and their mother carries them in this fashion with their heads alone visible. One thing we particularly noticed was that, whereas by far the greater number of goats turned aside as we approached and sprang up hill and down across the slopes, through the scrub, and even through thorn bushes to avoid us, this little mother with her burden stuck to the path. Sometimes she would tremble with fright and press closely against the face of the rock, but never once did I see her risk the safety of the young ones on her back by playing any dangerous tricks. An interesting subject for the psychologist. On the watershed we meet the rearguard of the flock, a shepherd carrying a small goat, his wife heavily laden and with an infant at her breast, and four or five children, of ages ranging from four to ten, trailing along after them whistling and calling to the sheep that follow them eagerly.

Up here for the first time since leaving Simla we get a fine view of the Shrikan Dhar and through the glasses recognise many old acquaintances among the snowclad peaks. The path by which we here descend the hill is exactly like the dry bed of a cataract, so much so that I shall never understand how our little cavalcade got down without breaking the mules' legs. This was succeeded by a twenty miles' walk along the Sutlej—the word 'walk,' I need scarcely say, implying something very different from a stroll in Hyde Park. Now the path leads us through the loose sand on the edge of the river bed, now some hundreds of feet above the gully of the foaming torrent. But it is interesting all the time. Sometimes thick forest runs down to the river's edge; sometimes the ground rises into mountain pastures. Or else the path will lead along the face of a cliff, and at the very point where you most need a rail or a parapet you will find a crumbling edge. But after all, no one who suffers from dizziness will ever reach this point; he will have tumbled head over heels into the Sutlej at a much earlier stage in the journey. So we get plenty of variety and some shooting into the bargain, which is needful as we

THE YOUNGEST PUPIL OF THE OPEN-AIR SCHOOL

(*Face p.* 142.)

FLOATING TIMBER

have to do our own foraging. Nearly all the inhabitants here are Brahmins who, not being meat-eaters, will neither keep fowls nor allow them to lay eggs. Luckily we are able to shoot a few pigeons, small but tender, and the sport anyway helps to pass the time as we go along.

Besides this, the banks of a large river are an unending source of enjoyment. There is always something fresh to be seen. To-day there are balks of timber floating down stream in great numbers, most of them huge sleepers of deliciously fragrant cedar wood. They come tearing along, shooting round the bends of the river and bumping over the rapids. Then after lying for a while circling round in an almost stagnant pool they are drawn into the current again and off they go in mad career, plunging down the stream.. A redstart is taking a ride on one of these balks, flying up every moment to catch insects. And a little further on a magnificent kingfisher, perched on the top of a floating balk, is gazing into the water. A bird with black plumage, something like a blackbird, bobs up all at once out of the water, hops on to the timber, runs across it and jostles the kingfisher off. As the latter makes away flapping his wings the little bird dives down again into the stream. It is a 'dipper'—a singular little person. You will generally see him running from a sandy bank into the water and disappearing beneath the surface, to emerge on the opposite side and walk away calmly to a neighbouring stone. In a minute he will be running back again and quietly recrossing the stream, swimming like a moor-hen. Then another vigorous dive, and up he shoots out of the water and flies whizzing along close in front of you in a bee-line with a loud 'ti-ti,' 'ti-ti.'

Finally he darts under the water and disappears. Evidently a bird of resource.

We are now approaching the Pandoa Ghat, a small rivulet along which we have to go in order to reach the watershed, for the Sutlej at this point runs into a gully again and there is no path. *Ghat* is the name used here for a mountain brook. Though the village of Pandoa is marked in large letters on the map it actually consists of only three houses, and there is no shop, so we can get absolutely nothing. And we are in a part of the mountains where the map indicates nothing but footpaths among hills and valleys.

It is plainly the eve of some holiday, for a great washing-day is being held in the neighbourhood of Pandoa. Men and women are sitting together by all the streams, having the time of their lives washing their garments and—*honi soit qui mal y pense*—their persons as well. They first light a wood fire on which they heat the water in great copper pots or pans. We camped that night on the banks of a little river whose course we are to follow on the morrow, with the prospect of having to cross it twenty times or more, bridges in this country of bare feet being looked upon as superfluous luxuries.

are on the move again directly after daybreak, anticipating a hard day's climb. The road leads at first up a pleasant incline with lovely views at intervals over the valley, which now lies in a deep gully, now broadens out into landscapes clothed with rice fields and full of bananas and other fruit-bearing trees. But as we advance, the mountains on either hand gradually draw nearer and nearer to the river, and the broad spaces grow less and less, until in a few hours we are tortuously ascending by a mere strip of a track. Then suddenly the valley makes a bend, the oncoming water, deflected from its course, chafing rebelliously against the face of the bluff. Here the path crosses to the other side by a row of large stones set at regular intervals in a shallow part of the stream. These provide a fairly serviceable bridge, the only drawback being that two successive stones are under water and therefore treacherously slippery. The mules of course splash unperturbed through the shallows alongside. This kind of thing doesn't occur just once or twice but continually. In a single hour we have crossed a dozen times, and the further we go the more unbeaten becomes the track and the fewer the stones available. Instead of stepping across we are obliged to jump, and if that appears too risky a proceeding we have just to cross over without shoes or stockings and be quick about it, for the water is execrably cold, and walking barefoot over the detritus of the river bed is anything but a treat.

It is amazing how the mules with their heavy loads pick their way, often knee-deep, through the foaming water. They feel out tentatively with their slender hoofs and always know exactly where the footing is most reliable. They will even nose along the bank till they come to a suitable landing-place and then spring to *terra firma* at a bound. All the time the roads are becoming steadily rougher, the current stronger and the scenery more ruggedly wild. On one side of us is an almost unbroken succession of cliffs with wild date-palms springing from the rock-face like ferns. Real ferns too there are in abundance, and waving grass, and an infinite variety of plants bearing fruits with hooked and prickly spines that catch in your clothing, or with barbed prickles that penetrate to your skin. Horrid customers! Again and again we are compelled to stop and pick ourselves free, and I may add, not of thorns alone, but of other things less fit for ears polite.

We naturally have to keep an eye on what the mules are about. At a certain point the second in the line refuses to cross, and while the drivers are attending to him, mule number two, out of pure cussedness, misses his footing, and before I can look round is up to his fat belly in a pool. And, what is more, the water doesn't reach to the said fat belly alone but to the edge of my specimen box and the bag containing my rolls of films. Poor old 'Snuffy'—the same by the way who gives us such a high old time of it at night by snorting every three or four minutes. There he stands quite contentedly drinking. He snorts when he sees me. The mule-driver snorts too in his turn, and in two ticks has got 'Snuffy' once more to dry land. By this time the water is running out of my boxes, so we promptly unload and open them. Fortunately the tin linings have saved the contents.

A quarter of an hour later there is another incident. One of the mule men is just carrying the Mem-Sahib over a part of the stream that is too wide for her short legs to take at a bound, when a loud 'jo-ho' and shouts of laughter are heard proceeding from the front of the cavalcade. The foremost mule driver, a tall muscular fellow whom we had named 'Jack-in-the-Box' on account of his sudden bursts of energy, springs into sight round an angle of rock throwing up his hands in amusement. We hasten forward with visions of our baggage floating away downstream, or some other equally pleasing accident, and are brought up short against a mass of rock about five feet high, from which the stream is flowing down in an elegant cascade. The mules stand stolid and expressionless with their noses glued to the rock-face. Apparently the path has come to an end.

As leader of the party I make a closer inspection, and discover the remains of some piled-up stones, an indication that the difficulty has previously been overcome. A gesture is sufficient. Laughing and chattering, our five men instantly set to work, we ourselves helping, to roll big stones down from above with a shout. The rogues have all learnt the meaning of 'Stand away!' from our former mountaineering excursions. Between these stones we wedge smaller ones, and within ten minutes have built a stairway by which our trusty mules are able to scramble up, each with a load of some 130-170 lbs.

Then on we go again. Presently one of the mules runs between a tree and the cliff, and the two chests containing our provisions and cooking utensils go clatter-clatter down into the bed of the stream. Fortunately they are caught just above the water by the branches of a tree. The mule meanwhile, needless to say, walks on with a completely unconscious expression of anything toward. A delay of another five minutes is entailed while the chests are hauled up and lashed together again. But the men take it all in good part. This little game, by the way, is repeated two or three times, with variations galore.

At two o'clock, after six hours' hard going, we find ourselves close to the place where we have to leave the watercourse and ascend the watershed by an innumerable series of zig-zags. Within a quarter of an hour we have pitched our comfortable tents on a patch of greensward just above the stream.

Don't suppose, however, that our boys take a rest after the fatigues of this interesting journey. No sooner have they got the tents ready than off they go, the whole lot of them, helter skelter down the hill. In another moment they are out of their trousers and into the water. Here they collect a lot of twigs and sand, and in a trice, before I have grasped what they are up to, they have dammed up a suitable spot in the river with a small opening at either end. As the trout try to get through, they catch them by hand, and before long Santoo is back again sitting before the fire with a sizzling saucepan. He holds a knife wedged between his big toe and the next, leaving both hands free, and draws the fish along the blade, removing fins and bones. These fried trout taste excellent and help to eke out a bit of meat from our camping supply. For pigeons are now becoming scarce.

Our ascent next day is by way of a steeply winding path along a south slope of black slate-stone. It is literally a case of " In the sweat of thy brow," and it costs us a hot stiff pull of a couple of hours to reach the pass. Crossing it we pass to the western slope. It is now close on twelve o'clock and the hillside lies exposed to the full rays of a burning sun, so that we are thankful for refreshment in the shape of water and nuts proffered by the friendly natives of a hamlet. Two more hours of this oven, mounting all the time, and the path finally turns a corner, bringing us rapidly to the first trees and at last out on to the northern slope into the cool shade of a magnificent pine-forest with abundance of rushing streams and a fine shady path running level along the hill. At the entrance to this forest a man is awaiting us. He has made a three hours' journey hither to get medicine for his wife who is suffering from malaria, and he has brought with him an offering of some most lovely apples. A real luxury after all this parching heat, and moreover a satisfactory proof of the efficiency of the mountain postal service.

It is gloriously cool, not to say chilly, here in the forest. An hour later the sky becomes slightly overcast, and by imperceptible degrees heavy clouds gather, so that when we make a halt for luncheon I involuntarily draw on a raincoat. In another five minutes we have the fire burning for tea and a second one lighted in the middle of the table among the plates, our table on this occasion being a large stone. And then all of a sudden as we are having our meal there comes a howling squall of wind, and down rattles the hail with a vengeance. Quickly we pile on more wood. The boys have lighted a fire more than seven feet in diameter, big enough to roast an ox. Here we wait half an hour till the storm has spent itself and then, the sky still remaining overcast, we pitch our camp in the heart of the forest on the only level spot we can find. There are deer about: we hear them coughing. There is also a cry of distant partridges. But our bag for the day consisted, alas, of nothing more exciting than sparrows! However, when one is hungry and a cold wind is blowing across the hills, even sparrows taste delicious. The next day we had nut-crackers for dinner! Our big game shooting was not exactly a conspicuous success.

Next morning I groped my way in the half-light to a fine

position I had selected over night at about half an hour's distance from the camp. There was a white frost on the ground and a nip in the air. Leaning against a rock on a grassy bank I sat contemplating the scene before me. At my feet lay the valley of a stream, its opposite bank densely wooded with a diversity of trees, and away on the right a clear view over our camp to the distant mountains where the stream has its source. The depths of the valley on my left are hidden by the grassy shoulder of the hill, but beyond it the eye travels over a foreground of mountain spurs right away to the snow peaks of the Shrikan Dhar, the furthest hitherward outpost of the Himalayas. Yesterday Traanberg had sighted several deer from this spot, running down the slope into the wood. And sure enough I had not been sitting here for five minutes when the game hove in sight. A spotted woodpecker leads the way. He has just the same markings as our own woodpeckers, but a golden head. On his heels come hurrying four nuthatches of two different varieties, and then a flock of tits, twenty or more of them and comprising four or five varieties. There are cole-tits like our own, but with white markings instead of yellow; there are tits half white and half yellow; others completely yellow except for a patch on the cheek; and one is a crested-tit with a pretty rust-coloured ring round its neck. After them come tree-creepers. These latter are precisely the same as ours.

For ten minutes or so the whole lot of them keep playing about a dead fig-tree not far from where I am sitting. They are presently succeeded by a flock of birds not unlike our wagtails in shape, the males with bright scarlet plumage and the hen birds a canary yellow. These are known here as 'minnevets.' In the East Indies they are called 'caterpillar birds.' Somewhere in the distance a partridge calls and is answered from four or five directions. The sun is now shining on the glaciers of the Shrikan Dhar and the darkness of the forest changes gradually to a dusky twilight in which the eye seems to detect the movements of shadowy forms. But it is merely an optical delusion. A deathly stillness pervades the whole valley. After a while the icy wind dies down, and as the sun comes out the grassy slope becomes deliciously warm. I linger for another hour watching all the birds that come along. A covey of five partridges sit sunning themselves for ten minutes or so on an old tree-trunk seventy feet above me; but I have left my gun at the camp alongside of the empty game-bag. At length I make my way back, pushing by a short cut through the forest till I come out into a field of wheat nearly two hundred feet above the camp, and there, just under my nose, freshly dropped and steaming, lies the dung of the passing deer! So much for my day's sport!

The next stage of our journey is downhill through the forest, with views at intervals over the deep channel of our tributary stream. This channel very soon becomes a deep gully into which we are forced to make a headlong descent by the most lamentably inadequate path, and discover on reaching the bottom that the gully unexpectedly soon broadens out till it scarcely deserves the name of a valley at all.

All the time we were going down we kept hearing the sounds of shouting and whistling in the distance and a commotion going on of a kind most unusual in these regions, consisting of knockings and rumblings that we could not identify. Presently we find that they are caused by numbers of wooden balks coming down the stream and constantly colliding with a dull bumping sound. A remarkable industry is being carried on here. In the early summer big cedars are felled in the forests above. Many of them slip as they fall and, being stripped of their branches, plunge by their own weight a good distance down the hill. Sometimes the woodmen avail themselves of the snow as an aid in getting the huge trunks down to a convenient spot where they start a timber-yard and cut them up into large beams, measuring on an average eleven feet in length by some fifteen to twenty inches in width and about twelve and a half inches thick. All this is done entirely with a hatchet. An awful piece of work, to say nothing of the waste of wood.

The trees thus being transformed into timber, they are carried by the coolies to a 'go-down' or wire-way, which conveys them to the bottom of the hill, or else taken to any stream handy that will answer the same purpose. And now the really curious part of it begins. Any attempt to float the timber is out of the question, the mountain streams being all of them far too shallow, and moreover strewn with boulders. Therefore a succession of gutters, or slipways, is constructed from the beams themselves, the water being conducted over them. The balks are then sent gliding at a great rate along these gutters, which naturally involves a danger of splintering. So that wherever there is a waterfall, or one of the gutters happens to debouch above the surface of the water leaving an hiatus, a barrage is made, where a pool collects into which the balks can be plunged with safety. Here they pile themselves up, and men stationed by the pool guide them deftly by hand or by means of sticks into the next gutter or watercourse. When the last balk has been shipped off from the starting-place the gutters are broken up in succession and sent downstream one after the other in the same way, till the whole load reaches the main river for transport to the plains. But even here great quantities of timber are stranded on the banks and the gravel shoals by the gradual subsidence of the water, so that coolies have to be employed with rafts all down the river, going through the gullies and rapids if necessary, to prevent the loss of any balks. And yet, when all is said and done, only seventy per cent. of the wood ever reaches the factory in the plains. The rest, splintered in pieces, has disappeared. Nevertheless, the fact remains that £85,000 worth of wood is annually delivered at the faetory from Bashahr alone. For this the Rajah receives some £6500, which will probably be doubled before long.

We follow the course of the stream for a good distance, springing from balk to balk, leaving the mules to go by a dreadfully stony path about seventy feet or more higher up, on the limestone level. The stream has worn itself down to the underlying granite, but the actual point of contact between the two strata is scarcely anywhere visible. Only once did we find banks of slate some feet in depth and full of garnets.

At the place where the valley broadens is a small village situated on a terrace. Here the rice harvest is in full swing. We had already seen it being cut further up.

This is, as usual, done by the women. In the present instance, however, they are all busy with the threshing, so the men have to step in. In one of the rice fields they have moistened the soil and stamped it down hard. When dry this makes a capital threshing-floor. Upon this they have spread bundles of rice, and four or five oxen are being driven round over them, a boy running screeching behind the sacred beasts addressing them with a cudgel. On go the great clumsy creatures, lumbering round in a circle, treading out the ears with their ponderous hoofs and occasionally taking a hasty mouthful as they go.

Presently the straw will be cleared away and the rice swept together and winnowed by the women, all of course by hand. The method is to scoop up the grain on a woven mat and toss it into the air for the wind to carry off the chaff. It all makes a charming picture of village life. The only drawback is that everybody wants to stop working to stare at the strangers.

And so we pass on our way, leaving this lovely spot behind us. Up hill and down dale we go, seeking shelter from a scorching sun in the pine forest or traversing the lean pastures of the shady northern slopes, down the course of one stream and up another, until at last after five days' tramping we reach Luri, about thirty miles from Seoni as the crow flies—or as they say here, "as the Bashahri goes," referring to a marked characteristic of the natives, who will never make a circuit round a valley but always cross it straight ahead.

In Luri we are once more on old ground, and here a surprisc awaits us. The rice which we saw planted out at the beginning of August is being harvested now in the last week of October; that is, barely three months later! In the field, alongside the one where the women are plying their sickles, is a crop of maize, and here a troop of five-and-twenty apes is busy on the sly. Whenever they are noticed and driven away each one of them makes off with three or four maize-cobs from which he has stripped the outer leaves. The beggars are as bold as brass. They seem to know they are 'sacred' and so have nothing to be afraid of. The damage they do must be enormous. Just think of the amount of that harvest that must be destroyed! Now there are pigeons bearing down upon it in flocks two hundred strong. They are beautiful birds but, alas, as gun-shy as the blacksmith in Rampur, who for ten rupees will make you a gun out of old bicycle frames which just take the regulation cartridge. These weapons look precisely like the popguns of one's childhood. Our friend can also make muzzle-loaders, but not flint-locks like the gunsmith in Algiers from whom I bought a pistol last Christmas.

Winter visitors keep arriving from Thibet. Many of these are men thrown out of work in their own country by the heavy snows. Besides the human element, there are also birds galore. Sparrows, larks, finches, yellow-hammers, hosts of thrushes, even ducks and cormorants, all come hither down the river seeking better quarters, while many of the summer residents, such as pigeons, drongos, and all kinds of song-birds, have already migrated south as they do with us. Some of these winter visitors are real beauties. There is for instance a redstart of steel-blue with a bright orange breast, finches with blue-black feathers on the back and strawberry-coloured breast and belly, and hedge-sparrows of all colours, from Turkestan and beyond.

All the valleys are full of autumn tints of red and yellow as with us at the beginning of October. Winter, alas, is approaching. But we still have a full month before the snow comes.

From Luri to Rampur we are on familiar ground, but we now make an invariable habit of spending the morning in crossing from one tributary to the next, generally a matter of six to eight miles. Then we pitch the tents, and employ the afternoon in walking as far as possible upstream so as to make acquaintance with the geological formation of the lower strata at a greater distance from the main river. There is granite-gneiss everywhere and garnet slate, and occasionally huge stretches of a white micaceous quartzite alternating with dark green or black hornblende rocks. All this entails a formidable amount of climbing every afternoon, mostly in the bed of the stream, because there we can get the best view of the lower strata and, moreover, can judge from the pebbles that have been washed down what we are likely to find further up. Exhausting work, but interesting withal, for you come to spots where the foot of man has never yet trod and where the beasts of the field are monarchs of all they survey. Constantly we are finding, in the wet sand, tracks of *goral*, the mountain goat of these regions, of panthers and martens, and very frequently of apes. On one occasion I came upon the remains of a half-eaten ape which a panther, disturbed in the midst of his meal, had left lying on a boulder.

All these streams are rich in bird-life. There are water-sparrows at every turn, and the great blue water-throstles nest in all the cliffs, birds with a peculiarly unmelodious note. Then there is our common yellow wagtail and a smaller one resembling our white wagtail, also a 'fork-tail' over one and a half feet in length. He really is a splendid fellow spotted black and white, and with regular wagtail airs and graces. But the most exquisite of all the birds is a white-headed redstart with a rust-coloured breast and a glossy black back, his little skull-cap being the only white thing about him. He is a bird of exceptional grace, not the least of his attractions being his very pretty note. This is all the more noticeable because, beautiful as all these birds are, there is not one to compare with our own blackbird or nightingale or black-cap, in the matter of song, or even with our own hedge-sparrow.

One more superb bird I must not forget to mention—the spotted kingfisher. Would that I could describe him adequately. He is a large bird, bigger than a pigeon, spotted and striped all over in black and white, with a black beak of portentous size and a crest that would make a hoopoe green with envy. The hoopoe, by the way, is yet another of our show pieces. He frequents the lower valleys and we sometimes find him on the grass-plot before the tent. On the higher levels and by the mountain streams he is never found, but you may often see him in the plains of India and even on the lawns of the public parks.

We had a lot of bother, by the way, over the spotted kingfisher. Our friend Mr. J., the ornithologist, possessed but a single specimen of this bird. Apparently it breeds somewhere far away in Thibet, only coming down to the lower streams in the autumn. J. had therefore begged us to do our utmost to secure him another specimen. The first one we saw was darting like an arrow down the Sutlej. Hopeless to try our luck with him. The second was sitting on the opposite bank and no amount of stone throwing would induce him to budge an inch from his place in the sun, far less to come to our shady side of the river. A third specimen we spied, perched on a rock affording a splendid mark, and well within range. I took aim and fired. Whereupon our coveted prize was off in a flash, the shot merely scattering harmlessly from the face of the rock. A little later on I had yet another chance which anyone might have thought a 'sitter.' But the only result of my shot was that the kingfisher gave one indignant glance in my direction and flew away. This bird is provided with immensely thick plumage as a protection against the cold of the icy water into which it is constantly plunging both in summer and winter. I should think I must have just missed hitting the bird a score of times at least; anyway I failed to bring him down. Finally, on one of the very last days of our tour, I managed to get hold of a superb specimen by a shot in the eye from my walking-stick gun at 60 yards. This bird is now in the Zoological Museum at Amsterdam, Mr. J. having in the meantime been fortunate in securing another specimen.

So there is always something of interest on the road. One day there will be chameleons, so-called at least. In reality they are lizards, with a comb of formidable dimensions on head and spine. The throat and breast of this creature turn a vivid red when it is irritated, which—*pace* all good Hibernians—has earned it the sobriquet of 'the

Irishman.' Another day there will be plants with great barbed seeds, horridly adapted for catching in the coats of passing animals. Which leads me to call attention to a curious fact. Among all the thousands of sheep that we came across, never did I find a single one with these seeds in its fleece. In the same way, I have never seen the seeds of the hart's-tongue fern in the coat of any healthy rabbit or dog. But sick rabbits and dogs, shooting dogs and others, sometimes have their coats full of them. In their case Mother Nature seems to have made no provision against the activities of these burrs. How it may be with our sheep on the Texel dunes I don't know. But if they are seed-carriers I should say they must have degenerated under domestication.

The people we meet on the road are also worthy of attention, especially the coolies employed in the lumber traffic along the rivers. One broth of a boy I especially call to mind, with an engaging smile, a lovely set of teeth and a dandified coiffure, the hair being tied at the back by a band crossing the forehead. He had a magnificent brown neck and well-developed chest, and wore a necklace of beads of silver and red china with a blue and green enamel pendant set in silver. We sat on our heels together for three-quarters of an hour on a boulder by the stream bargaining with him for this ornament. Not a word of English or Dutch did he understand, but when I indignantly answered: "Nothing doing!" to his extortionate demands, he grasped my meaning perfectly. Our knowledge of his language, however, which consisted chiefly of numerals and a few words of command equivalent to: "Come here!" or "Look out!" proved amply sufficient.

Finally the business was settled, and my wife was only too ready to give him a few extra pennies for the sake of his beautiful eyes. Unfortunately the necklace did not make much of a show on my wife's bare neck. It may have a better effect on a high blouse of dark velvet.

Each valley leaves its pictures on the memory: Behna Ghat, Machhad Ghat, Behra river, Nogli Ghat, and many bits of scenery along the banks of the Sutlej, with the harvest at its height and the birds of passage busy on the shaggy hillsides. Kites and vultures still wheel overhead as in the days of summer, but with them now are numbers of eagles, come hither from their breeding places in Middle Asia where winter has already begun to deprive them of means of subsistence.

There is not much snow as yet on the Shrikan Dhar, and the nearer we get to Rampur the more evident it becomes that no rain has fallen since the last rains at the beginning of September. Everything is dry and parched right up to the foot of the glaciers, and there is a much larger expanse of brown rock showing up against the white of the snow and the icefields than was the case in July.

At Rampur great preparations are going on for the Annual Fair which is to be held in November, and all the roads are so crowded with mules passing to and fro that we get away as quickly as we can, having one more large side-stream to explore before we finish our programme. This stream lies on the opposite side of the Sutlej, which until quite recently formed an almost insuperable barrier between the states of Bashahr and Kulu. Even now travellers seldom cross the river to visit Kulu, for the good reason that they have to raise their own transport coolies, a job which on this side of the Sutlej is always undertaken by the Government.

However, this presents no difficulty to us with our mules, and so on the morrow we make an early start for Kulu.

CHAPTER II

FROM RAMPUR TO KULU

THE ascent is by a tolerable path though exposed to the sun. Directly we cross the Rampur bridge we find ourselves in a new country Clothing, ornaments, articles of daily use, all have a peculiar stamp of their own, a relic of the time, not fifty years since, when it was impossible to cross the river hither save at the risk of one's life.

Now, of course, there are signs and advertisements everywhere, and all the shops have for sale the same lamps which are such an eye-sore in the bazaars of Bombay and Travancore. But the costumes are new to us, an especial novelty being the headcloths of the women, which are held in place by fillets of silver. The necklaces too are unusual. These consist of silver beads, made from four-anna pieces beaten into hexagonal shape, alternating with blood-stones made of porcelain.

A coolie is approaching. He has two objects dangling on his breast which on closer inspection prove to be a tooth-pick and an ear-pick of silver, prettily wrought and set with rough turquoises, the silver being the work of the local smith while the turquoises came from Thibet. In exchange for the sum of one rupee these trinkets are soon transferred to my wife's watch-chain. (*N.B.*—After a good preliminary bath of permanganate !)

Presently there is a thudding of footsteps and round the

corner comes trudging a damsel with a basket containing a dozen or more rugs of woollen homespun. It so happens that we are needing something of the kind for a door to the servants' tent, as the nights are getting chilly. But it ends by the young woman selling us two of her copper pins as well, thereby reducing her modest habiliments to a state so suggestive of the Venus de Milo that I feel constrained to present her hurriedly with a couple of safety-pins to veil the sight of her charms. She is a comely lass, and wears her tooth-pick and ear-pick, this time of wrought iron, attached to a wire ring, in company with her corn-cutter and a pair of tweezers. This collection we also add to our spoils. These little instruments are of especial interest, being exact counterparts of those I found in graves of the bronze age in the northern provinces of the Netherlands: pins, ring and toilet instruments complete, together with a fibula similar to that illustrated on page 164.

Our next encounter is with a shepherd. He parts with a beautiful copper-mounted tinder-box at such a price as makes his wife insist on selling us her necklace at the weight of the silver, plus one rupee. A good bargain, for the pendant was a fine example of native work, blue and green enamel on silver. It had the usual representation of the goddess Kali the Terrible, but with the addition of a pretty ornamental border.

The women have an interesting way of fastening their necklets. These are not suspended in the usual fashion in a plain circle around the neck and over the bosom, but have the middle piece caught up a little by two strings, thus allowing the silver beads on either side to fall down in a kind of festoon. I commend the idea to our jewellers. (For the patent rights apply to my publishers.)

Beguiling our way in this fashion with small purchases, we manage to accomplish the twenty-four miles and the ascent of 6500 feet which lie between us and Sarahn, within a space of two days.

At Sarahn we set up our headquarters for four or five days in a glade of the pine forest at the foot of the mountain, where the only tracks are those made by wild game. We are greeted while pitching the tents by the welcome sight of a covey of pheasants flying overhead. No need therefore to feed on sparrows this time. Every day now we get pheasants or partridges, with an occasional snow pigeon by way of a change. The snow pigeon is another rare bird which only comes down to inhabited districts

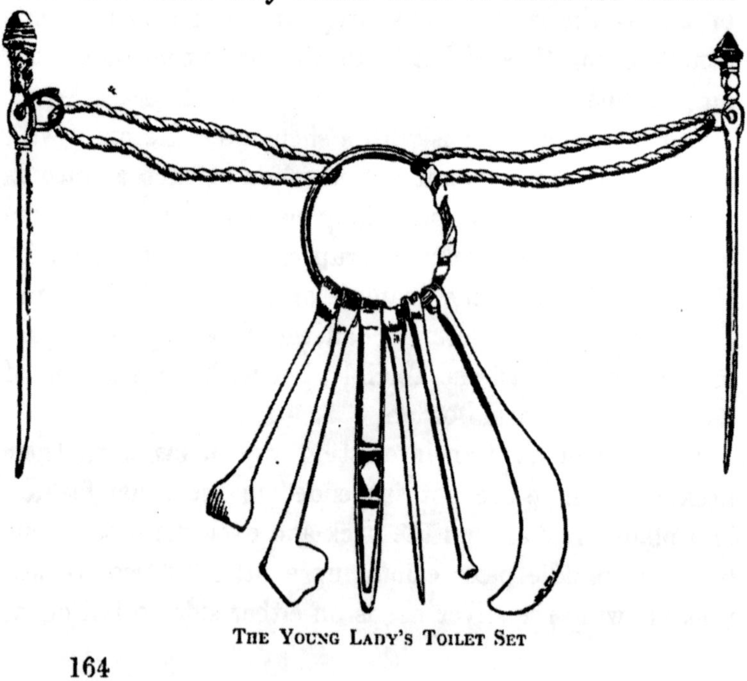

THE YOUNG LADY'S TOILET SET

during the winter. We preserved the skin only for our collection, the drumsticks being always removed by the cook. These birds arrive in flocks of two or three hundred at a time.

Winter draws on apace. When Santoo brings our early tea, everything is white with rime, and at a later hour there is still ice in the wash-basin. But we have plenty of wood, and throughout the day there is bright sunshine. The only drawback is that the days are so short, for we have still a great deal of work to get through. Our first exploration of the Khurpan Ghat revealed the presence of such varied stratification that we feel compelled to follow up the course both of the main river and its tributary for a certain distance. This is really what has brought us to our quarters in Kulu.

We begin by taking a day off, which means reconnoitring the neighbourhood at our leisure. We are now at an altitude of over 9500 feet. There is abundance of game about, and it is evident from the habits of the birds that it is seldom or never shot. For instance, if you shoot a pheasant the partridges come to see what you are up to. There is other game as well. About twelve o'clock while I am busy writing letters I hear a great uproar in the pine-woods above, the predominating note being a loud shout of "Ho-ho!" "Ho-ho!" Seizing the rifle from our kit, I go slowly up the mountain-side in the expectation that the din above will send some interesting head of game charging down the hill. I take up my position discreetly concealed behind a boulder on a ledge of rock whence I can get a view into two valleys, and have not been there five minutes when there is a rustling among the foliage on the hillside and then a thud as of an animal alighting after a spring. Then rustle, rustle, bump, bump! The sound rapidly approaches till it is on a level with me in the valley on the right. I get ready, as a dark shadow appears, rustle-rustle-bump-bumping down the hill, and automatically raise the rifle to my shoulder. When—tableau! Out into the open space darts a shepherd dragging a dead sheep by the horns!

I fear that my remarks, though in Dutch, were uncomplimentary. Seeing my look of inquiry the shepherd informs me that the sheep has been killed in broad daylight not 1600 feet above our camp by a leopard. Alas, I regret to say we saw nothing further of the latter, for although we delayed our departure in order to pay a visit to this near neighbour of ours we drew a blank through ignorance of his address. It was really a nuisance.

On November 8th our exploration of the stream brought us up above tree-limit to an altitude of about 12,000 feet. It happened in this way. At a distance of only a quarter of a mile beyond the camp we were obliged to forsake the direct course of the stream for the simple reason that it brought us up against a precipice at least 160 feet high, down which its waters gushed in a magnificent cascade. The rocks rising amphitheatre-wise around a heap of detritus brought down by the torrent afforded us no chance of a foothold. Therefore, to overcome the obstacle, we had to make a détour to a spot whence a steep path led by zig-zags up the side of the slope, and continuing high above the level of the stream brought us to a mountain pass bridging the watershed of the Indus and the Sutlej and leading into Kulu proper. I should here incidentally remark that though the district in which we have fixed our camp is, politically speaking, reckoned as part of Kulu in consequence of the impossibility in former days of crossing the river, it actually belongs geographically speaking to the Sutlej valley and the state of Bashahr.

Following the above-mentioned path we get back to the river through alternating stretches of grassland and woods of pines and ilexes. Pheasants are calling everywhere, and once we start some deer. The forest grows denser, and at last when further advance is becoming laborious we find that the river has now narrowed to such an extent that there is no further prospect of its yielding anything of interest. Besides, it is again flowing through the old familiar grey granite-gneiss. So we struggle back in the direction of the path.

Luckily we come across next to none of those hooked seeds which are so plentiful in the lower valleys. Wild roses there are, also a bramble with tremendous prickles, and a poisonous kind of *berberis*; but these all grow in the form of shrubs with gaps between so that you can pass through. There are cedars too, and numbers of ilexes, their branches covered with trailing lichens like those you see on the damp northern slopes of the Bavarian and Austrian Alps. On the edge of the forest the familiar sight of eagle's feathers, lying about in immense quantities, shows that we are nearing the head of the pass. This lies saddle-wise in a depression between two peaks, the more northerly of which is only a few hundred feet above us. So we decide to climb it.

The first thing we notice on the high levels near the summit is the great dearth of bird-life, in contrast to the woods below where pheasants and pigeons, tits and woodpeckers abound. Once above tree-level all bird-life ceases. It is very different in the summer. Then there is dead silence in the recesses of the forest, while up higher, the mountain slopes swarm with birds : redstarts, blue-breasts, orange-throats and red finches. So it is plain that winter has now arrived and that the birds have migrated south.

We toil laboriously upwards among the rocks where the *Sedum crassifolium* is growing in great tufts, the same plant that one sees in so many of our rock-gardens at home, and presently we are ascending the southern slope with the grateful warmth of the sun on our backs. At length we reach the top, and are suddenly rewarded with a panorama it is worth coming many weary miles to see.

In the foreground rises the most southerly spur of the Shrikan Dhar, known as Khand Mahadev or ‘ the seat of the most high god,’ so called from its being the place on which Parbati the spouse of Shiva spent a whole year in supplication for the blessings of motherhood. To the right of this happily designated spot is a series of snow mountains ; then comes the gap of the Sutlej valley, and beyond it are our old friends Raldang and Jistingrung and Kailas, whose enchantment we experienced at close quarters when at Chini. It does one's heart good to behold them again.

On the other side rises the familiar form of Mt. Hattu, whose ascent we made in June. From our present standpoint we obtain a much more imposing view of the snow mountains further west gradually ascending till they culminate in a monster peak whose declivitous sides fall sheer away to the blue of the distant plain. In these we recognise the Zaskar range and the giant peaks of Nunkun. At yonder point the Himalayas veer to the north, letting in a vista of far Kashmir, land of fertility and flowers, the earthly paradise of our dreams.

But after all we are not so badly off even up here, and have much to interest us besides that vision of the world of snow. For behind us the mountains flow gently down to the valley of the Sutlej, and our eyes fondly seek out Seoni and Pandoa and Luri and Kepu with many another nameless spot of good and gracious memory. Moreover the sun is shining from the clearest of skies, and on the flat mountain-top there is a basin in the rock clothed with high grass, an ideal place for a nap which we take full advantage of. And this, mind you, in the beginning of November at an elevation of 13,000 feet! Who could foresee that only four days later the place would lie three feet deep in snow?

The drawback to a mountain top, however, is that you can't as a rule remain there for long. The Swiss Rigi and Stanserhorn are exceptions, but then they are not really mountains, properly speaking. So we retrace our steps. By this time it is well on towards evening. We therefore make a short cut. As there are no paths in this wilderness, we have to scramble down as best we can by dint of sliding and jumping for nearly 3000 feet, passing traces of pheasants and deer, and in one place the marks of where a bear has clawed up the moss on the hillside. Then we regain the path and are able to descend more rapidly.

From an angle of rock a plump partridge flies up right in front of me. As it recedes I send a charge of shot after it. It gives a little flutter and drops behind a boulder.

I cross the stream and pushing through the scrub go to the spot where I saw it fall a little way up the hill, when, peeping cautiously round the rock, I behold a marten surreptitiously making off with my partridge in his mouth. Hearing me coming he runs in among the rocks. It is a ridiculous sight. Presently he lays himself down upon a projecting ledge and begins his meal, starting operations by violently shaking his prey till the feathers fall about my head. There my fellow-murderer lies sucking his fill of warm blood until three stones aimed in his direction cause him to withdraw out of reach of my wrath. Former experience has taught me that to shoot again would be sheer waste of powder.

On rejoining my wife I find that Santoo has lit a brisk fire in the middle of the path and is roasting some apples so that we may have something warm to get our teeth into as it is growing dusk and rather cold. A little rest and refreshment by the way are most comforting when one has been afoot ever since 7 a.m.

The next day we go to the village intending to do some shopping, but behold there are no shops! Everything that is wanted has to be fetched from Rampur, a good two days' journey. We soon discover, however, that the inhabitants are very resourceful and self-dependent. They all make their own clothes, and for their ornaments and the copper pins with which their garments are fastened they have recourse to the village smith, just as our forefathers used to do in the old Franconian days. Those who lose their pins, and cannot afford new ones, make shift with porcupine quills, which are fairly common hereabouts.

I have previously mentioned that the women wear a peculiar kind of black headcloth confined by a silver fillet. The nose-ring also is peculiar, being in the shape of a Turkish crescent, but a quarter-, instead of a half-, moon. Several rings are worn on the toes, a thing unusual in

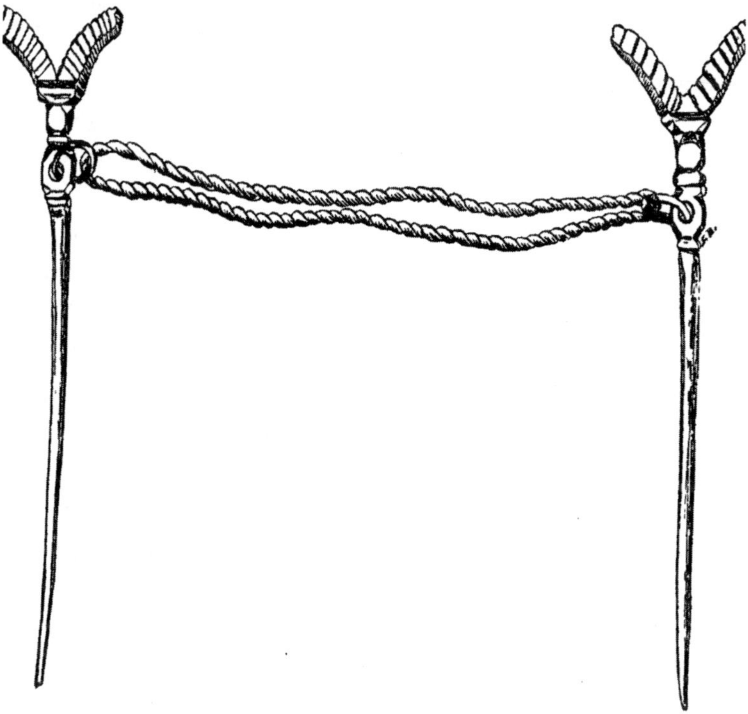

PINS USED BY THE KULU NATIVES FOR FASTENING THEIR CLOTHES

Bashahr. But all this by the way. A point of more importance, so far as we are concerned, is that there is not a single lamp in the village, so that we can get no oil for our lamps. In the wooden houses all the light is supplied by means of torches made of long slips of pine-wood of exactly the same pattern as that employed 2500 years ago in the old salt-mines of Hallstatt, as instanced by remains I myself have discovered.

The village temple is also of quite a different style from those met with elsewhere, being of lofty elevation and built almost in the shape of a square pillar with projecting balconies on the upper storey. The carved doorway struck me as particularly primitive in execution. In front of the temple we saw a man busy setting up a rug on a loom, while on a balcony a little way off his companion was sitting spinning, the spindle gripped between his toes.

It is very entertaining going round a village of this kind. Everybody seems quite prepared to see us, having been warned of our arrival, and instead of running away they all go on calmly with what they are doing as if nothing unusual had occurred, though the mayor of the place, an old man of seventy or so, told Santoo that so far as he knew no white man had ever been seen in the valley before.

Our next object is to have a look at the upper reaches of the Khurpan Ghat. This means an early start, as to reach the river we have to cross the intervening mountain ridge. This excursion being totally impracticable for the mules, we send them down the hill by the way we arrived, a track dignified by the name of a mule-path but in places much more like a spiral staircase or the shaft of a mine. They are to wait for us at a given point.

When we start, the grass is still white with rime and there are fringes of ice along the banks of the stream. There is a cold sting too in the air, but this gradually yields to the warmth of the sun.

Our path is one of those laid down by the Forest Department. It scales the face of the cliff that rises behind

A GUARDIAN OF THE TEMPLE

(*Face p. 172.*)

HOW THEY SPIN

A VULTURE

Sarahn and in some places slants at an angle of exactly forty-five degrees as measured by my gradient metre against the tree-trunks by which it is underpinned. But it is splendid walking along above the tops of the pines and cedars that have rooted themselves into the fissures of the rock, with lovely views over the wild scenery of the hillside whose every crevice is filled with trailing shrubs and red with the glory of autumn tints. The depths of the valley are veiled in a regular autumn mist. Plumes of blue feathery smoke rise from the village below, the resinous smell of burning cedar-wood lending an additional sting to the frosty air. There is a dead silence only broken at intervals by the tinkling note of the tits or the twitter of the golden-crested wrens, the same cheery little creatures that enliven our own pine-woods in winter.

A climb of two hours brings us to the crest of the mountain and in a few minutes we see Khand Mahadev shining forth in all his majesty above the pine-trees. Then we make a slow descent through tracts of wild jungle with open glades at intervals, bearing all the while to the north in the direction of the Khurpan Ghat, which issues from a ravine a few miles further on. To make a circuit round the upper reaches of the stream would take us a week, that is of course including the journey there and back, which is more time than I dare risk with winter so near at hand. So we go straight down the steep side of the ravine and make for a village lying on a terrace above the stream. Through the glasses we can see the cobs of maize hanging to dry under the eaves of the houses. A further fact is also revealed, namely, that our winding descent is being watched by thirty pairs of eyes in the village of Jaun just below, where a group of figures is seated on the market-place. It looks like a school, and such it proves to be. As we jump down with a rush from the last slope on to the market-place the whole class rises and salaams, the teacher in broken English bidding us welcome in the name of the Municipal Council. The said Council, a few ragamuffins of forbidding appearance, likewise rise and salaam, bowing themselves together like so many clasp-knives. They are assisted in this performance by the ladies of the community, one of whom, by the way, has on a golden breast plaque worth at least £25.

"Wherefore are the Sahibs come?" they ask.

I reply laconically and with effrontery:

"To inspect the school. Where is the school house?"

"We have none," announces the master. "It is much healthier in the open air."

"But if it rains?"

"Then there is no school."

"And in winter?"

"Oh, we have no school in winter."

What a country! Where else could you find such a curriculum or such holidays? I recommend that these methods be brought to the notice of our educational pundits.

We next proceed to examine the pupils, who seem to have some idea of English history and geography, though they make an even worse hash of words like Southampton and Edinburgh than do the children in our primary schools in Holland. Then the youngest member of the class, a newly breeched infant of six, steps forward and rattles off the multiplication table as fast as any of our own school-children can do.

I tell the master to let the children resume their work, and then inform him that we are Dutch people. That, however, is beyond his comprehension. We are white and therefore we must be English. I endeavour to explain that there are other countries near England, just as Thibet is near Kulu. He listens attentively and then inquires if Holland is *quite* close to England, being obviously relieved when I reassure him on this point. Before leaving we make a final round of the school. The children—they are all boys of course—sit on the ground with their legs crossed under them. Each has an earthenware ink-pot of village manufacture and a couple of pens, not made from goose quills but from bits of bamboo. The ink is merely soot and water, and a wooden board whitened with chalk serves for writing paper. The boys go away to clean their slates, preferably in the gutter. Then more chalk is put on and they start again.

I call up the eldest pupil and hold out to him a box of lucifers. No, he has never seen such a thing, and is dumb with astonishment when I strike a match. And then the young rascal produces from his girdle a tinder-box, a very primitive affair, but it does the trick. I allow him to look into the reflex-camera. Again he is struck dumb, and so is the schoolmaster. But when the members of the Municipal Council also come crowding round, it is time to stop. We have already noticed some of these gentlemen scratching themselves, and we know but too well what that means. . . .

On the village green is a tent occupied by a native official of the Forest Service. We had spied him from above sitting smoking a gigantic hookah while his servant was busily engaged pulling on his socks. But apparently his lordship has fled at our approach; so we just linger a moment to watch some oxen threshing out the grain and then resume our descent of the hill.

Here let me mention, by the way, that this hamlet, which has no building available for the government school, possesses none the less a temple measuring 160 ft. × 325 ft. It houses a community of some dozen priests, which is possibly the reason why there is no money forthcoming for the school!

By this time we have reached the stream which flows in a prettily wooded channel, the path running first on one side of the water and then on the other. Bridges there are none. But what matter? It is always warm in the sun in the middle of the day. The pheasants are calling in the underwood, and the autumn tints are glorious. The whole expedition is more of a pleasure trip than anything else, only rather a long one. By the time we get back to camp that night we have actually been on the tramp for twelve solid hours. The expedition, however, has resulted in the investigation of a goodly number of crystalline rocks, and we have brought back with us also some amusing photographs of the district and the village school, besides gathering a fine bunch of narcissus blossoms in a water-meadow by the stream. Narcissus in November! We must try to grow this variety in Holland.

The next stage of our journey after leaving Sarahn takes us uphill and down again by a sharp gradient to Rampur. As we approach the town an unusual bustle is apparent, to-morrow being the day of Rampur's great Annual Fair, an event of world-wide importance. At this fair Thibetan ponies are exchanged for the ginger of Sirmoor, and Yarkand clothing for Patiala rice. Here, too, great stores of costly wool from Kulu and Bashahr pass into the hands of traders from all parts of India, who pay for them with the dirty brown sugar brought hither from Kalka and Simla on the backs of innumerable mules.

A Kulu Necklet

CHAPTER III

RAMPUR LEVY AND THE SNOW

It is the 11th November, the date from time immemorial of the great Annual Fair in which South Thibet and Nepal, Bàshahr and Kulu all have their share. It is pouring with rain and thousands of drenched people are camping out in the streets and the public squares or under the trees and the overhanging rocks. The river is rising steadily at the rate of several feet per hour. Brooks become streams; new brooks arise and flow right across the road or, what is worse, both over it and along it. Perhaps I should not say 'worse.' As a matter of fact I never saw Rampur looking so beautiful as it did on the second day of the Fair with a broad stream of water nearly ankle deep in the main street. It was not until the third day that the clouds, which had obscured the valley, at last lifted disclosing the mountain summits clothed in snow down to a level of seven thousand feet. The dense pine forests were a glorious sight in their winter garb of snow.

We had taken up our quarters in the garden of a large villa placed by the Rajah at the disposal of his guests. On two previous occasions we had stayed in the villa itself, but one part of it was now occupied by Mr. C., the same Deputy Commissioner who was of such assistance to us in Simla, Mr. K., the Head Ranger, being installed in the other part. Fortunately we found a good sheltered place in the garden where our baggage was safe from the attentions of light-fingered gentry. No sooner had we arrived there than down came the rain in torrents. Our tents luckily held out splendidly, so that we were almost sorry when, on the second day, Messrs. C. and K. came to say that they had cleared out a sitting room and bedroom for us in the house and that their servants would help us move in. Still, although one may quite well put up with getting wet through every day, it is no laughing matter to have no chance of drying one's clothes when one comes in. So we accepted the kind offer, little dreaming that this was to be the end of our camping-out, at any rate for the present. When we next moved on we had to travel for days together through snow two to three feet deep, so were only too glad to make a friendly compact to share the rest-houses with Mr. K. who accompanied us.

Before leaving Rampur we wanted to pay a final visit to the Fair, the devastating rains having so far made camera work more or less impossible. It was the last day and there was a great rush going on, so that no one had much time to spare for bargaining and still less for talking to strangers. The people themselves were most remarkable. I noticed that many of them would draw back in alarm when brought face to face with me or my wife in the crowd. These were nearly always the natives of the Mongolian type, the men and women dressed almost alike and both wearing long plaits of hair. They were covered with turquoise necklaces and had their ears and their fingers loaded with rings. Here and there, I am glad to say, we met with some more confiding specimens of humanity who gave us the opportunity of buying a few of their ornaments, each party naturally bargaining without understanding the language of the other. During these transactions we would be encircled by a whole crowd of natives laughing and cheering though not understanding a word we said. But I always knew when I had paid too much for anything by the kind of articles that the spectators would instantly offer me at the same price. It is a remarkable fact that the Thibetans do not even know the numerals in Hindustani. All their reckoning is done on the fingers, using the whole finger just as we do, and not the finger-joints after the ingenious method of the Arabs who count up to twenty-eight in this fashion, and as they generally leave out the two joints of the thumb they have an exact two dozen literally ready to hand.

THIBETAN PRAYER-WHEEL

Most of the people in the crowd wear top-boots of woollen material and the men from Lahul and Leh a blue peaked cap turned up with red. These latter gentlemen are terrified to a degree by my camera and dash away down side alleys in a panic directly they catch sight of me. The same thing happened in the case of a solemn Lama priest from Lhasa. He was coming along at a dignified pace turning his prayer-wheel when suddenly he espied us. Off

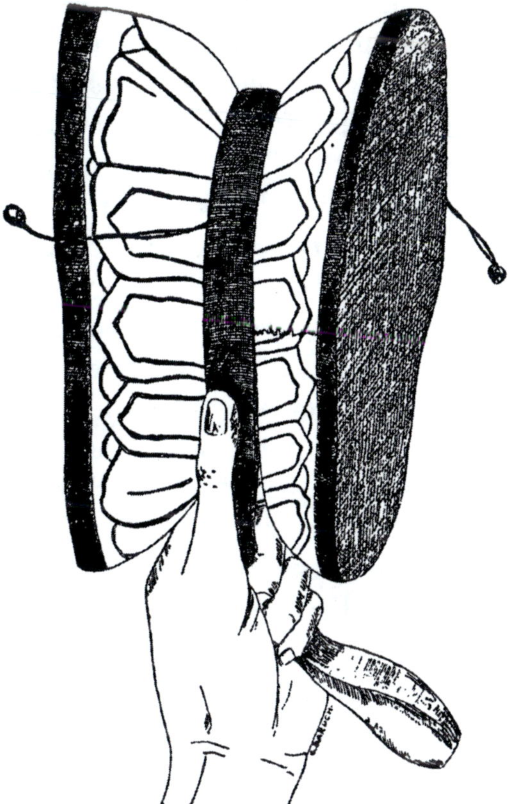

Lama Priest's Drum made of two Skulls

he ran immediately at a brisk trot, hiding his relic under his clothing and drawing a cloth over his head to protect him from that most pernicious of weapons, the evil eye. I had another try the following day, when I discovered that a sort of alarm service had been instituted. One man actually imperilled his immortal soul by running to our camp and keeping an eye on our tents! This was rough luck, but fortunately I came across a whole lot of priests a few miles further up the road who were quite friendly, and even prepared to give us a performance of sacred music. Their instruments consisted of a silver bell and a drum. These formed the accompaniment to a combined sighing forth of "O-ohm," the name of the divine power omniscient and omnipresent.

The leader of the party was carrying the family-god on his back in a copper shrine and he offered to sell it for seventy rupees, probably the highest numeral the rascal was acquainted with. The bell, they declared, was not for sale. The drum, however, apparently was, since it was transferred to my possession. And a remarkable specimen it proved to be. Most of these drums are round in shape and made of wood. They are shaken to and fro by a handle causing two weighted cords attached to the sides to strike the tympanum. The special characteristic of my drum was that it was made of two skulls. Skulls of unbelievers undoubtedly, for all the faithful departed here are committed to the fire. Moreover, skulls of Christians, not Mohammedans. A pleasing reflection that perhaps two foresters or missionaries may have given their heads to provide this Lama with a new drum. This lugubrious instrument has decorative lines scratched all over it and is mounted with bands of red and green. Its tone is clear and pleasing.

None of all this seems exactly to tally with the teaching of the Buddha as we understand it, *viz.*: "Peace on earth and the comfort of man and beast." Rampur is a centre of Buddhism in Bashahr. The Buddhist temple of the district is here In it is a great prayer-wheel seven feet high and over three feet in diameter. It is adorned with letters engraved on copper, just like the smaller wheels of which we managed to secure specimens by dint of money and fair words. There were also prayer-rolls for sale, long printed strips for putting into the prayer-

"O FATHER SATURN, I BESEECH THEE, GRANT ME A CHILD."
Tankri Inscription on a Prayer-Sheath

wheels. The high priest could not tell me what was on them, being unable to decipher the Tankri characters. Anyway they were genuine, having been printed in a monastery in Lhasa and cost five rupees the set. These strips containing special petitions are also worn in prayer-sheaths of silver and copper, and are considered of great efficacy, though, given the illiteracy of the priests, there is reason to suppose that a woman may sometimes be found in treaty for a fine flowing beard or a man for the blessings of motherhood!

I won't make your mouth water by an inventory of all the treasures that were for sale at that Fair. Suffice to say they comprised products from Kashmir and Yarkand, from Turkestan and Thibet and Nepal. So you can sympathise with a poor retired schoolmaster like myself who had not the wherewithal to take full advantage of so unique an opportunity. Nevertheless I managed to bring away a great many more things than I can give the public any idea of in my restricted number of illustrations.

In the afternoon I went with Colonel C. to an audience of the Rajah, who had called at the bungalow that morning. The crowds at the Fair having got wind of our official visit stand thronging the road to watch our august progress. On the steps of the palace we are met by the Rajah, who bows profoundly and mutters "Salaam," for he doesn't understand a word of English. He precedes us to a sort of bandstand where he takes his seat in a red plush armchair facing an enormous mural painting of the Buddha surrounded by a host of gods and demons. We are meanwhile bidden to a place on the sofa, a piece of ancient furniture whose threadbare condition is judiciously masked by red silk draperies heavily embroidered in gold thread. In front of the potentate stands a golden salver of colossal dimensions bearing a monster teapot, a couple of flasks, and something that looks like a sugar basin, all of solid gold. When we are comfortably seated the Rajah begins by taking some perfume in a golden spoon from the golden pot and putting it on to Colonel C.'s handkerchief. I happen to have a silk handkerchief in my own regalia, a souvenir from a lady friend. This also is treated to a dash of the liquid, with the subsequent result that my wife banished my whole costume from the bedroom! The Rajah next scrabbles in the great golden pot and presents us each with a handful of something that proves to be cardamon seeds, luckily without their skins. These when chewed impart an agreeable odour to the breath. One wonders whether this is a precautionary measure rendered necessary by the sort of guests he sometimes receives?

No politics are to be discussed during this visit, His Highness having intimated as much beforehand. So after a few preliminary platitudes he beckons to twelve attendants, each of whom advances with a big silver salver. On the salvers is the most extraordinary assortment of articles I have ever beheld. One tray is full of silver rupees, another contains one pound's weight in gold, another has figs, a fourth rice. There is a woollen blanket on one tray, a silken headcloth and a piece of unbleached calico bearing the mark of a Liverpool firm on two others, while yet another tray bears a single egg, and so on, and so on. All of these are presents to the representative of the British Government, most of them of course having a symbolical meaning. The Colonel points to the silk headcloth, which his servant folds up and removes, and the guest having made his choice the remaining things are cleared away. This silk cloth has to be handed over by Colonel C. to the Government to be placed in the Treasury, no state official being allowed to receive gifts from the native princes.

The comedy being now over, the Rajah takes us round his new palace, which has been in the course of building for the last ten years. At the present moment the work is at a standstill, apparently owing to lack of workmen. It is harvest time, and people are far too busy on their own land to do any work for anybody else. But when the slack season comes workmen will automatically reappear. The funniest thing in the palace is the telephone box with an installation enabling the Rajah to ring up his palace in Sarahn. Beyond this he can do nothing with it, for there are only these two installations in the whole of his realm and there is no connection with Simla or the rest of India.

The palace contains a new throne wrapped up in a dust-sheet. It is upholstered, like the armchair, in red plush and its arms are adorned with gilded lions' heads. The Rajah is very proud of it. Unfortunately there are no windows yet in the palace, so that the rain has washed all the paint off the feet of the throne. But the glass is on order, so at any rate a move has been made in the right direction.

In the corner of the square in which the new palace is situated stands the old palace. This is an impossible rookery of a place and I should much have liked to peep inside it. But we hadn't a chance, for the Rajah now advanced to the door. The guard—six men strong—presented arms, and we took our leave, accompanied by His Highness to the bottom of the steps.

Walking through the narrow lanes and alleys, still crammed with people, we arrive at the villa to find the floor of our rooms covered with gifts sent by the Rajah. Chickens, vegetables, potatoes, rice, sugar, salt, fruit, dates and figs, while bleating outside on the terrace is a magnificent ram. Welcome supplies all of them for the days that lie ahead. We are hard at work for the rest of the day getting them all packed, for on the morrow we are to continue our journey.

This is more easily said than done. We are now about ninety-five miles from Simla, and of this distance more than sixty miles lie at an altitude of 8000-9000 feet under two or three feet of snow. But, as I always say, what costs nothing is not worth having, so we start off determined to make the best of it. C. and K. accompany us, one for shooting and the other on business. They precede us on horseback in the drizzling rain, for the weather is still unsettled, and when we overtake them later they are knee-deep in sopping grass with a whole lot of beaters driving partridges. Thanks to the shoot there is no trouble about dinner for one day at any rate. Presently the weather improves a little and a few gusts of wind clear the view. We turn into a road along the Nogli Ghat, a tributary stream facing the Khurpan Ghat, and in a short time have mounted hundreds of feet above the Sutlej. Gradually the clouds lift and at a bend in the road we suddenly get a clear view away over the Khurpan Ghat to the rocky precipice of Sarahn and the forest above the village where our camp stood. The meadows and the mountain summit higher up are all thickly covered with snow. It is a mercy we did not stay on there a day longer. In the pouring rain we could not have got down without danger to the mules, and in newly fallen snow it would have been a sheer impossibility. We might have been kept there at least a week waiting for the weather to change.

We continue to mount. Towards noon the sky again

becomes overcast and by one o'clock when we get to the Taklech bungalow a violent snow-storm is raging through the pine-forest above, and the drifts are coming lower and lower down the mountain side. The winds howl about the log hut where we sit warming ourselves by a blazing wood fire, and in dry clothes, our mules having arrived soon after we did. With hot tea and a plum cake baked by Santoo from ingredients bought in Rampur and some I suspect borrowed of C.'s cook, life is once more worth living. The rest of the afternoon we spend in arranging specimens, making up diaries and writing letters. So the time flies.

Towards four o'clock the shooters arrive soaking wet, stone cold, and with a poor bag. Suddenly there is a tremendous hustle and bustle. The Commissioner calls from his nice hot bath for some fresh clothes and is informed by his servant, a first class ninny, that the mules have not yet arrived. The fellow had seen our mules outside the hut and jumped to the conclusion that the others were there too. To cut a long story short, his Honour then wriggles back into his wet togs and walks into the parlour with teeth chattering to warm himself by the fire, apologising for his toilet being dirty and covered all over with thorns and seeds.

Five o'clock comes but no mules. Six o'clock and still no mules. A relief expedition is then dispatched with lanterns and torches, an animated discussion in Hindustani being carried on meanwhile between the servants and cooks. Presently Santoo comes in to say that the two gentlemen who, by the way, had invited us to dinner, are beginning to wonder whether there will be any dinner at all. By this time it is plainly up to us to show hospitality, so we beg them to be our guests instead, and my wife holds hasty conclave with Santoo and Jittoo. We appear to have one tin of sausages left and another of corned beef, some onions and apples remaining over from the gifts of the Rajah, and a few potatoes Santoo has got on his own account. In addition there is our sumptuous plum cake and the ingredients for a rice pudding. It is only to be hoped that the other mules will turn up in time for the Commissioner's chocolate and bonbons to be served for dessert. There are also some 'stinkers,' our guests' elegant name for cigars, contributed by Traanberg who had bought them at Rampur.

At seven-thirty we sit down to table with beating hearts, our guests making a thousand apologies for their shooting clothes while we have gone to the opposite extreme and put on our best bibs and tuckers in their honour. Santoo and Jittoo are both as proud as peacocks and do the waiting admirably, keeping our guests' servants meanwhile ignominiously out of the room labouring under a sense of defeat.

At eight o'clock there is a trampling of hoofs. The caravan has arrived. It seems that one of the mules caught its load against the side of a rock and rolled right down to the bottom of the slope, the box bursting open and scattering the local archives, great and small, all over the wet grass. It had taken hours and hours to collect them. I can imagine the vigorous language of the unfortunate owner when he wanted later on to refer to his official notes.

Well anyway, the dinner went off capitally, including

the dessert. We sat talking for a while afterwards and our guests arranged a party for the morrow to shoot *goral*, in which Traanberg was included. We ourselves would be busy making a geological survey of the neighbourhood.

That night I was waked by a tremendous bang as if a door had been slammed. At the same instant I felt my bed move out some five or six inches from the wall. Then I heard Traanberg's voice calling out: "Yes, I'm coming." Apparently he had realised at once it was an earthquake and was up in a jiffy before any of the servants came to wake him. Getting outside he found it was only three o'clock instead of six as he had thought. The rest of the party were apparently used to such things and went off to sleep again.

Next morning we are informed that the road higher up is totally impracticable for the mules. But as K. is travelling with coolies he starts off, being in a hurry. I prefer not to risk any accident to the beasts, so decide to wait until he sends word what the road is like and what the weather conditions are 3000 feet higher. Meanwhile there is enough collecting to be done in our present surroundings to occupy us easily for another day.

The reports from K. later proving favourable, we continue the ascent by way of a good broad road which very soon brings us to snow covered pine-woods. Then after mounting for 3000 teet or so, the road passes over to the western slope, which is here clothed with a variety of timber, many chestnut trees amongst others, out of which jays and apes, as well as deer, seem to suck no small advantage. These creatures provide us with a good deal of diversion during a tramp of several hours. There is only a thin coating of snow in the forest, but when we get out on to the grassland it has increased to a depth of nearly two feet. But by this time the sun has begun to come out and we lunch at an altitude of 11,000 feet amid the snow in a grassy glade in the middle of a thick cedar forest, lighting a big fire to warm ourselves and making tea with snow water. The path next takes us down a very rocky pitch of the northern slope where the snow lies about three feet deep. Fortunately it has been trodden down to some extent, for in another minute the sky becomes overcast, masses of grey cloud rise up from the valley beneath and it starts snowing hard. A bad look-out, as we have another two hours' walk to tackle, and the sky grows darker every moment. Fortunately a squally wind comes to our aid, driving the bulk of the snow behind us so that only a small portion falls where we are. But it is icy cold, so we make all speed to reach the Bali bungalow, the mules arriving soon after we do. Man and beast at once get under shelter and all precautions are taken against the impending storm.

At this place we overtake K. and sit talking together over a friendly meal of tea and cake. Our conversation confines itself almost inevitably to the weather. We discuss the winter which has begun so unconscionably early and wonder what chances we have of getting home by Christmas. Suddenly, as we are talking, there comes another awful squall of wind shaking the whole house and the door bursts open, letting in a red glow through masses of driving snow. We move to the threshold. Before us shines the red splendour of the sun, sinking to rest behind a distant ridge in a streak of orange and gold, melting away on either hand into the faintest azure and crowned by masses of leaden clouds. As we gaze, the radiant streak broadens and fades, and on coming out again after supper we find the moon shining brightly. It is freezing hard and all about us the pine-woods and fields gleam white under the newly fallen snow. On the far side of the ravine a grand range of mountains rises silent and majestic against the swart blue of the sky. All the old familiar peaks of the Shrikan Dahr stand out distinct in the moonlight. There is promise of a fine sunrise on the morrow.

Next morning we are out before daybreak. It is bitterly cold, the thermometer registering only 14° Fahr. The air is crystal clear. Away on the horizon where the wan blue overhead pales to a pearly white, the snow peaks flash rosy in the dawn, gradually detaching themselves in blanched and sparkling radiance from the russet verdure of the valleys, and the ever increasing blueness of the sky. A mighty panorama indeed, for Bali our present halting-place stands on a mountain promontory with the valley at its feet.

It is still piercingly cold when we begin our march, for we are afoot soon after sunrise. But our path to-day runs almost level along the southern and south-easterly slopes from which the snow has in great measure departed. The wintry temperature too is an excuse for increasing our pace, so that the distances seem shorter than usual. We also have the pleasure of K.'s company. As he has travelled all over this part of the country on Forest Service business for the last five years, he has plenty of adventures to relate. Besides occupying the chief official position here, he is generally the only Englishman to be found in the district and therefore is often called upon to undertake jobs outside his special province. Last year, for instance, he received a telegram from the Superintendent of the Hill States, the local title given to the Commissioner, Colonel C. The contents of this telegram, brought by a coolie who had come a four days' journey with it, were short and to the point. "War between Bashahr and Gahrwal. Go and see what you can do."

In four days, by dint of forced marches, K. reached the place indicated, a mountain ridge forming the boundary between two states. Here a great commotion was going on. On either side of the frontier line were assembled a hundred men and more. Fighting, however, had not yet begun. K. pitched his camp and sent out a message to the chiefs of both parties, bidding them present themselves the next morning at ten o'clock. But when the hour arrived he was paying for his hurried journey by a sharp attack of fever and was only able to give orders that no one was to leave the valley till he was better. His illness lasted for ten days, during which time the hillmen met, smoked, and talked matters over, with the result that when they finally assembled for the big Council all pugnacity had abated. Nevertheless, the affair had to be enquired into. It then transpired that some sheep belonging to a Bashahri had crossed the mountain to graze in Gahrwal. The said sheep being observed by a Gahrwali he gave them a bit of his mind in the shape of a charge of shot, and the Bashahri shepherd who had come in search of his errant lambkins had a near shave of being struck by a ricochet. Whereupon a report flew to the next valley that he was wounded, and in the next two valleys he was given out as dead. The further the news travelled the worse it became, until on arriving at Rampur it had assumed the form of an armed invasion of Bashahr by Gahrwali cattle-stealers. The Rajah instantly mobilised his bodyguard of six men, called the rest of his subjects to arms, ordered them to concentrate on the frontier, and gave the finishing touch by dispatching a courtier to Simla to invoke the help of the British Raj.

K. got the men to discuss the matter quietly. The alarmist reports were traced to their source and a promise was exacted from the Bashahri, the author of the whole disturbance, that he would look after his sheep better in future. Finally K. drew up a treaty of peace which, signed by the local chiefs and witnessed by himself, was sent up to the head of the government in Simla!

But no sooner was he back at his quiet job of counting trees and marking timber, than an acknowledgment of his above-mentioned services arrived in the shape of another telegram: "Frontier dispute between Kanet and Kunmarsain. Try to keep peace."

Again K. lays down his hatchet and goes off. A three days' journey brings him to the part of the frontier in question, above Kepi and Luri. He summons the chiefs to his tent and finds that it is a case apparently of a ruction over the irrigation of some rice fields. He suggests going to see the place the next morning so as to settle the dispute. No, the Sahib must on no account do this! Why? Because they are fighting at that spot to-morrow. "Very well," says K., "I'll come up and inspect both armies to-morrow morning at six o'clock, and don't you dare start fighting till I have done so."

At the appointed hour K. arrives to find a disorderly rabble of woodcutters, a good hundred and fifty of them, gathered round a number of fires. He addresses the first man he meets in fluent Hindustani: "Well, and what are all you fellows doing here?" "The Chief's orders," is the reply. "But what are you all up to?"

"Fighting!"

"And where are your arms?"

The answer to this is that everyone has got his hatchet and some have a kind of hay-fork.

"And whom are you fighting?"

"Those lazy dogs of Kaneti."

"Where are they?"

"Why over there sitting by the three furthest fires. And a few of them are with our own people round the other fires."

K. thereupon goes and stands upon one of the dykes between the rice fields and delivers himself as follows:

"O men, it is well that you have come hither. But your help is not needed. Go to your homes in peace and let each return to his own work. Quick! March!"

He himself remains behind with the two chiefs, settles the matter according to his discretion, and thus war is averted. And all this in the year of Our Lord nineteen hundred and twenty-five!

I merely record these things to show you what still goes on in remote corners of the British Empire, and as an illustration of the great effect produced by peaceful intervention on the part of a European. The British Raj rules indeed over a remarkable set of dependencies. It is world-wars like these, of which no newspaper takes cognizance, that give one the best idea of the curiously mediaeval conditions still prevailing in the country.

These and similar tales so beguile the way that we put on a spurt and easily make the dâk bungalow at Sungri before sunset. All the same it is a good pull up, for Sungri lies on the watershed of the Ganges and the Sutlej where an icy blast is blowing, and the last part of the way we have to climb about 600 feet up a northern slope covered with snow to the depth of three feet. So it is good to be welcomed on arrival by a blazing fire. K., who travels with about a dozen coolies, is accustomed to send them on in advance under the direction of one of his servants. So afternoon tea is ready on the table, and when K. invites us to share it we notice that his bed is made, that his shoes and slippers are sorted out into pairs, his evening clothes ready folded, and even his writing-table in model order with lead pencils, pen, ink, and stamp-box complete. It's rather depressing to see that ship-shape and orderly writing-table. It gives one the cold shivers down one's back to think of having to get back to work again oneself instead of sitting comfortably in a corner of your tent, your legs crossed under you, and all your worldly goods, wife included, lying about anyhow in elegant confusion.

زبان

CHAPTER IV

THE END OF THE JOURNEY

We had left Colonel C. behind in Taklech. In Sungri we parted from Mr. K. and continued the journey with our own staff. Everything seemed very dull and quiet after the crowded activity of the past days. The ground was frozen hard and, worse still, over two feet deep in snow, so we had to have our wits well about us as we went along. In the middle of the road occasional travellers had trodden down a pathway about a foot in width. This had half thawed and frozen over again during the night, so that down the centre of the track there was a ridge of ice ten inches high flanked by the two feet of snow. On this ridge we had to walk. If we slipped off it we sank in over our knees. And what the poor mules had to put up with may be imagined when I mention that the surface of the melting snow had frozen into layers of ice so sharp that it lacerated their hoofs. The consequence was they kept falling about perpetually and it entailed a regular *tour de force* on the part of man and beast to get them up again. It generally meant unloading the animals. But they all seemed instinctively to realise that it was imperative to push on at all costs. The weather at present was glorious, but at any moment it might play us false and cause a repetition of our experiences of November 11th, in which case we should be cut off from the outside world for a considerable time and without sufficient provisions. As a matter of fact the winter snow did begin ten days later and, I may add, is still blocking the road as I write these lines on April 27th. K. was returning by the tributaries of the Ganges, and Colonel C. going up the Sutlej valley, so that we were actually the last travellers to approach Narkanda along the upper road 7500 feet higher by way of Kadrala and Baghi.

Kadrala ! Would that I could describe that wonderful spot. From a deserted hut on the mountain ridge one looks away over the surrounding cedar-clad heights to a distant view of the snowy Himalayas, ranging from Pir Panjal to where Badrinath rises grander and more imposing than ever. And then the walk through the cedar-forest in all its winter glory ! We had of course some hard days going. Let anyone who has not forgotten his college training try 'legging it' all the way from London to Dover in broiling sunshine, with shoes in holes, and with drenched feet. Then he will have some idea of what we had to endure. It is surprising how hot one can get in the open on the snow. But the cold of the pine-woods is really awful. It was freezing hard there all day and the snow in places lay to a depth of more than three feet. However, if one wasn't warm one could soon become so by working away at removing the trees that had fallen across the road and were a great hindrance to the mules.

But how beautiful it all was ! The forests and mountain-slopes covered with snow, and above all the distant view from the ridge with the winding path in the foreground. And that far-away world of ice and snow, so far away and yet, in the clear winter air, looming so close at hand under the hard blue sky. A fairy vision and yet a stern reality! Who can ever forget it—that view from Kadrala? Two hundred miles away, and dominating the entire landscape from its sublime altitude of 23,000 feet Nanda Devi arrests our fascinated gaze. So austerely remote are these bare and lofty mountains, and yet so one with the all-embracing universe, that mighty and mysterious Oohm transcending the divinity of Vishnu himself, that what marvel the Hindu should here behold the dwelling-place of his gods.

The sun dies down in the west. The mountains flash with rosy light. And high aloft great Nanda Devi glows like a lighted taper. O Brahma! O sun born of the lotus flower! O glory of the dawn! We yield thee thankfulness for this day.

For a fair and gracious day it has truly been. By the time the sun has set and Nanda Devi has gleamed its last farewell we have once more reached the watershed. All day long we have been following the snowy track along the north-eastern slope overlooking the valley of the Parbar, a tributary of the Ganges. Now we recross to the Sutlej side of the ridge and make for the next bungalow, three or four miles further on. The twilight is short here, but there is bright starlight and a full moon is rising, while every available particle of light is reflected from the snow. The forest in the snow has a weird beauty of its own but it presents odd difficulties, as we have to pass over and under several fallen trees. We try as far as possible to move away these obstacles to let the mules get by, so that it is eight o'clock by the time we reach the rest-house and eight-thirty before we can rouse the caretaker from the effects of his first winter carouse. And our poor mules, who have had a terribly heavy day of it, don't turn up till ten. However, we have reached our goal, being now close to the highway, the familiar Hindustan-Thibet Road which will remain open for another fortnight at least for postal service and the transit of sheep and goats from Thibet and Spiti.

The next day's march to Narkanda is a good long one. A lovely day, sunny and warm. The pinewoods are full of tits, and there are apes astir everywhere. At Narkanda we are met by Job's tidings. The Rajah of Kunmarsain, who was to have organised a big shoot for us, is prevented from doing so. So we have to go on to Matiana along a road fairly free from snow. Then, as we still have one or two tributaries of the Ganges, more especially the Giri, on our programme, we don't proceed at once to Simla, but, taking a sharp turn just after leaving Matiana, we go down more than 3000 feet to the stream.

Down there the difference of temperature is enormous. We have migrated from winter into late summer. There are pink mallows in bloom and a luxuriant growth of tobacco, bamboos and bananas, and all kinds of plants with which we have become familiar in the lower valleys of the Sutlej and the plains of Tropical India.

What a joy it is to be able once more to choose a spot and put up our tents in the evening sunshine, and after lingering a while over the fire to turn in early to bed in the dear old tent under the starry heavens!

We spend a day or two thus, wandering through tracts of desert scenery where the giant euphorbia grows in dense profusion, sometimes walking by the side of the river, sometimes mounting high above it, or occasionally going a little way through the stream when the ravine is broad enough for us to pass along under the rock-face. And it is interesting all the time. One never knows what one may find round the next corner, and we are always blissfully uncertain of the hour at which we and the mules, who have to keep to the road, will reach the appointed camping-place. In this happy land of Patiala there are neither highways nor milestones, and here in the hills it is always very difficult to estimate distances by the map. Moreover, the tracks by which the mules have to go are none of the best, and once at least we nearly had a bad accident. One of the mules, which had two boxes containing food and kitchen-utensils slung across its back, knocked against the side of the cliff, lost its balance, and rolled over down the hill. All that could be seen by the horrified spectators above was first a box, then four floundering hoofs, and then another box, rotating down the slope. Finally this rolling monstrosity went smack against a tree more than 700 feet down and hung there with splinters flying in all directions. After some deliberation we decided that it might be as well to find out whether there were anything worth saving. So the boys descended the slope gingerly step by step to avoid being smashed to atoms themselves against a tree. I accompanied them with a revolver to put the faithful beast out of its pain if need be.

On our approach 'Snuffy,' for it was none other than he, made an effort to rise, but in vain, as he had no support for his hind legs. From a hurried examination it appeared to me that he was completely uninjured, his fall having been broken by the boxes. These however had not fared so well. The box with our provisions was in smithereens. Jittoo carefully gathered up a potato here and a handful of rice there, but the whole ten pounds of sugar we had just laid in was streaming downhill in a sort of waterfall. Through the glasses I could just see a tin of salmon—our last—bounding away down to the botton In short, there was no more salvaging to be done in that direction. The box with the cooking things was still whole but had assumed the form known to mathematicians as a parallelopiped, with the result that two of our forks had gone slap through the bottoms of three aluminium saucepans. The rest of the things, however, were still usable. As there was already a great chunk out of the lid of our stoneware teapot that of course had escaped further injury.

How my fellows ever performed the superhuman feat of getting that mule up the precipice is a mystery to me. It must have been by alternate pulling, pushing and carrying, or all three combined, unless something may be put down to the intelligence of the mule himself. Anyway, up he came, and arrived in camp looking as bright and brisk as any of them, though for the first time in his career he was four hours late.

But really on the whole we were very lucky with our animals. When I mention that in a journey of three weeks you generally reckon on one mule out of four coming to grief, mostly through the carelessness of the drivers, and that we lost none in a month, it will be admitted that we were indeed fortunate both as to men and beasts.

We spent several more days wandering about the mountains and the beds of the streams, finding everywhere the same deposits of dreary grey-blue slate that you meet with at Simla. But there was abundance of plant life and there were hosts of birds. Especially striking were the multitudes of vultures. An infectious cattle-plague was raging in the district, killing off dozens of zebus and buffaloes. The dead animals are generally dragged to the edge of the precipices and flung over, and on each of the carcasses you will find some thirty vultures gorging themselves. Strange uncouth creatures they are, with ugly bare necks protruding from a splendid collar of down. Nevertheless, on the wing these birds are distinctly handsome and their flying powers are in no way inferior to those of the Himalayan eagles. A flock of such vultures would frequently accompany us for some distance, apparently on the look-out for an accident. A pleasant idea when one is scaling a precipice!

The next portion of our road was through Sirmoor. This is one of the smaller Indian States, which has recently come into notice through having its own postage-stamps just as Patiala has, though I must confess I never came across any of them, nor could I find a post office wherein they might be bought. I made enquiries in every village we passed, for I am an ardent philatelist, but in vain, and the one and only time I ever had to send a letter from this district I entrusted it to a mule-driver. Most of the traffic here is by way of the mule paths, and the Government has little or nothing to do with it; for there are no forests to be felled and the land both in hill and valley produces little more than is sufficient for the natives themselves. I must make one exception however, namely, ginger, a commodity exported by the State in large quantities. In every village we meet with caravans of ten to thirty mules all laden with this ginger, of course in its raw state of dry twisted root stocks only worth about a halfpenny the pound. It is all taken to Solon, a small town on the Kalka-Simla railway, which controls the entire trade of the foothills, and the mules return with loads of sugar or salt. This traffic makes the highway so crowded and dusty that, even were we not obliged by our researches to follow the footpaths along the streams, we should prefer to do so despite the steep gradients and the constant circuits.

We spend four days in Sirmoor and another four in Patiala. The number of vultures keeps steadily increasing, and when we pitch our tent above Kargamu on the Giri we find a religious function has been fixed for that very night for the purpose of imploring the gods to stop this plague.

Meanwhile I made one last excursion through the bed of the Giri. The stream at this point is over 300 feet wide, and comes nearly up to one's waist in places, so that my servant and I were frequently in danger of being carried off our feet by the current, which we had to cross eight times to avoid being held up by sheer walls of rock. We were fortunate in killing a big tawny vulture for our collection, but it was so fat that we found it impossible to preserve. One wing alone cost us a whole afternoon, and it took three men to get the skin off. The spread of the wings from tip to tip was over seven feet. These creatures are of colossal size and have huge hooked beaks and stubby talons very different from the elegantly murderous weapons of the eagle and the owl.

That same evening preparations were made for the night of intercession, if I may so call it. Large quantities of fuel were collected, the first fires lighted, and the drums and tom-toms laid around to dry. For nearly an hour they kept tuning up, till at last I enquired when the gods were coming, and was informed that only Rama and Shiva were to be invoked on this occasion, as local gods had nothing to do with cattle-plagues and such like. The function was to consist entirely of singing and ceremonial dancing and would last from midnight till six in the morning.

Meanwhile we had stoked up a fire of our own and amused ourselves by watching the various types, many of whom recalled those we had seen at the Tara Devi festival near Simla, only they were more slovenly in appearance. After dusk the crowds increased. Devotees from all the surrounding hills were summoned by roll of drum and 'ti-oo-oos' from the long temple trumpets. For the more the suppliants, the greater the chance of a favourable answer to their prayers.

Night comes on. All along the hillside move wandering points of light, and the crowd around the blazing fire grows larger every moment. It is a motley crew of dirty, slatternly people, the women as usual covered with ornaments. Eight o'clock comes, nine o'clock, ten. And still the throng grows denser. Still the lights keep wandering along the hillsides. The ceremony won't begin till midnight; and the village gods will have no part nor lot in it. Meantime we ourselves have a ten miles tramp behind us, and so—to bed!

The hum of the crowd and the muffled sound of the drums ebb and flow, lulling us quickly into unconsciousness. We are soon fast asleep. Presently—Do I wake or do I dream? What is it? 'Wireless'? Surely I know that tune? The motif is quite familiar. What on earth is it? Why, of course! *Les contes d'Hoffmann.* Offenbach's *Barcarolle.* That's it, sure enough! Only, sung over and over again like a kind of dirge by a vigorous male voice. And in every line I catch one word: '*Ramayana*'! A Brahmin is chanting passages from the sacred books, strophe by strophe, to the accompaniment of a drum. And the melody he sings is that which Offenbach is said to have borrowed from an air he once heard the sailors humming in some seaport town.

Then other voices join in, and some lines are repeated in chorus. But the motif is always the same. At last I fall off to sleep again, waking at dawn as the last lights are being extinguished on the hillsides.

Everybody assures us that the road to Solon is one of the best. And the distance about eight miles; some say ten; others say twelve. But anyway they all declare it is no more than a day's march, and again assure us that it is the best of roads.

And so indeed we found it—a nice broad well-beaten thoroughfare. What our informants omitted to say was that one has to cross one of the main tributaries of the Giri no less than eight times in three hours, and of course without a bridge. Little details of this kind are not thought worth mentioning. Also the distance to Solon turns out to be fourteen miles instead of twelve, with a climb of 3000 feet half-way. A good day's march indeed! However, we have safely accomplished all we set out to do and can now look forward to Christmas at home.

THE END OF THE JOURNEY

Only a few days remain, three of which we spend in Simla packing and taking leave of our friends, and as the motor purrs along the road bearing us back to Kalka and the plains, and Simla recedes into the distance behind us, we recall the moment when with gay insouciance we turned our backs on this outpost of civilisation to fare forth into the wilderness, with its myriad marvels of plant and animal and human life.

And as each turn of the winding road brings us nearer the valleys and the great plains of India we keep asking ourselves the involuntary question: Shall we ever see those giant mountains and those strange peoples again?

At Kalka we bid farewell to our faithful Santoo, who has waked us every morning, brought us our early tea, and cared for us like a mother during our four months' wandering in the wilds. He can scarcely be induced to leave us and looks tearfully from the window of his departing train as the Mem-Sahib presses into his hands a few apples for the journey.

Then on again we speed through the vast expanses of the plains and finally, after one hectic day in Bombay, still hot though it is now December, we embark on board the liner for Haarlem.

And this, mark you, gentle reader, is but a fortnight's voyage, which brings Narkanda within three weeks of your own fireside.

So if, because unread before,
You doubt the tales I tell to you,
Go, travel forth to yonder shore
And see if what I say be true!

THE END

INDEX